T0209038

BROKEN

My abduction story

Sky Sparrowhawk

BALBOA.PRESS

A DIVISION OF HAY HOUSE

Balboa Press books may be ordered through booksellers or by contacting:

Balboa Press
A Division of Hay House
1663 Liberty Drive
Bloomington, IN 47403
www.balboapress.com
844-682-1282

Because of the dynamic nature of the Internet, any web addresses or links contained in this book may have changed since publication and may no longer be valid. The views expressed in this work are solely those of the author and do not necessarily reflect the views of the publisher, and the publisher hereby disclaims any responsibility for them.

The author of this book does not dispense medical advice or prescribe the use of any technique as a form of treatment for physical, emotional, or medical problems without the advice of a physician, either directly or indirectly. The intent of the author is only to offer information of a general nature to help you in your quest for emotional and spiritual well-being. In the event you use any of the information in this book for yourself, which is your constitutional right, the author and the publisher assume no responsibility for your actions.

Any people depicted in stock imagery provided by Getty Images are models, and such images are being used for illustrative purposes only. Certain stock imagery © Getty Images.

Print information available on the last page.

ISBN: 978-1-9822-6618-9 (sc)
ISBN: 978-1-9822-6620-2 (hc)
ISBN: 978-1-9822-6619-6 (e)

Library of Congress Control Number: 2021906660

Balboa Press rev. date: 04/21/2021

CONTENTS

FOREWORD

It is an honor to be asked to write this foreword. Sky writes her life story and experiences in the hopes of inspiring others to work towards their healing. She is an intergenerational survivor of the Canadian residential school system and was kidnapped at a young age. Sky also experienced violence, addiction, homelessness, unhealthy relationships, and sexual assault. She has allowed herself to be raw, vulnerable, and to share her truth, so that the reader can either relate or begin to understand how trauma impacts a person's thoughts, feelings, and beliefs. I am humbled by her resilience and strength.

Despite her experiences she relied on key cultural teachings, prayer, key people, and counselling to help her through the most difficult times in her life. Her message is clear: each person can learn to feel safe, to feel connected, to trust self, and to build healthy relationships if there is a will and an effort made by the individual. While this was not easy for Sky, she never gave up on herself. In my opinion, she is not broken, as the only difference between us is our experiences. She is not damaged goods, but rather a precious gift from the Creator. I encourage people from all cultures and backgrounds to read her story.

ACKNOWLEDGMENTS

There are people in my life that I would like to thank and acknowledge in this journey of life. First, I would like to thank my daughter for leading the way in my healing. I thank my husband for creating a safe home for me to heal. I thank my mother for never giving up on looking for me. I thank my father for guiding me in love to the Creator. I thank my Auntie for encouraging me to write my story. I thank my Granny for her love and support. I thank friends from work who took the time to hear my story and offered kind words and support. I thank all the counsellors who helped me in my healing. I thank my brothers and sister who encouraged me to keep going when I felt like giving up. To Charlene, thank you for all your prayers and blessings. To my friend Claire, your love and humour helped me through many hard days. To Marilynn, your empathy has healed me in ways you could only imagine. To Zip, you are a champion among men! Thank you Zip for knowing when to advise, and when to listen. My wish for my supporters is that all the love and support you gave me goes back to each one of you, tenfold. To the Creator, all the tears I cried, I knew you were with me. I felt your presence. Thank you to the Creator for helping me through some exceedingly difficult times. I know there were moments that you carried me.

PREFACE

I have prayed and continue to pray to the Creator to help me heal from the painful childhood I survived. I know Creator guides me to forgive those who hurt me and to also forgive myself. I have spent a lifetime trying to forget horrible and traumatic experiences. I want to forgive myself for the choices I made along the way. I continue to pray and work to release myself from the pain and perceived hatred inflicted upon me as a child. I ask the Universe with the utmost respect, to love and accept me as I am. I give myself permission to feel the uncomfortable memories and experiences of the pain, so that I can move forward in my healing. I pray that one day I can love and accept myself unconditionally and believe in my heart that I am not 'damaged goods.' I feel that I must now stop and walk through the fire and continue to walk forward. Creator, I pray that you let the hell that continues to torment me in my body and mind to fall away like ashes.

I have shed many tears remembering the pain and suffering I endured as a child from key people: one of these key people was my mother. As a child, I believed my mother's rage would one day kill me. As an adult, I now know that my mother was tormented by her own 'demons' stemming from the Canadian Residential School system. Over time, I learned to reduce my mental and emotional pain. I became an 'observer' of my past life, so that the memories and experiences would lessen their intrusion into my daily thoughts and feelings.

It was not until I suffered a breakdown as an adult that I was able to really connect with the emotional turmoil of being kidnapped at the young age of eleven. I was held captive by 'Kirk' for eighteen months, another key person who caused much suffering. Going back to this point in my life helps me understand the events that shaped me, the 11-year-old girl and the adult woman I have become. I have learned that the road to forgiveness is treacherous. I have heard the phrase that 'the hardest person to forgive is yourself'; this I know is true. I have worked for years to forgive myself, and to release the pain associated with the kidnapping. I carried a host of emotions for many years, including guilt and shame. I acknowledge that my guilt served as a driving force, pushing me to work hard to overcompensate for the shame I carried. I felt guilt, shame and puzzled in my decisions to go along with my kidnapper, Kirk.

Several years ago, I knew that I needed to forgive myself. I had no idea how to forgive myself but knew that I carried a great deal of anger. I yearned for peace and happiness, but my thoughts and feelings betrayed me with anger, doubt, shame, guilt, and self-loathing. I prayed to Creator to show me how to forgive myself. The Creator heard my prayer one day while I was in a health and wellness store. I came across a CD and booklet that advertised teaching forgiveness. The instructions were simple; I was to connect with the feelings of the violation. This seemed simple enough for me at the time. I then bought a magazine that profiled ten documented kidnapping cases. I also bought a Bob Segar CD, the one with the song, 'Against the Wind.' (My kidnapper played this song. Throughout my life I was not able to listen to this song without having a panic attack.) I naively thought the forgiveness exercise would take me an afternoon or maybe even a day, so I planned a day. I drove out to a lake, read the magazine, and listened to the song 'Against the Wind.' I allowed my feelings to come and cried uncontrollably for hours. For the next few days, I tried to pull myself together, but I knew that I would need to sit with these feelings a lot longer. I felt I could not forgive myself until the intensity of the emotions subsided. Little did I know that there would be much more work for me to do to forgive myself. I had opened pandora's box and it would be months before I could sleep more than two hours at a time. I do remember that I experienced white flashes of light many times just as I was waking up. I would jump out of bed feeling terrified and anxious. I had descended into a dark, fearful place. My overwhelming emotions wouldn't allow peace or rest for days. When I cried, I felt I could not stop and that the crying would never stop. Thanks to the Creator I had mental health counsellors to support and help me through this period in my life.

As you read my story you will notice there are a lot of gaps, I don't remember all of it, and that's ok. I spent many years beating myself up, and I tried so hard to forget. The fact that he was never caught, also weighed heavily on my mind. I have lived a fear-based life, but I chose to let it go, and free myself. I was kidnapped at age 11 for 18 months. This is my story based on all the facts I can remember. The places names and dates have been changed. There are many graphic details contained in this book and I recommend any persons reading this to seek professional counselling services, should they find themselves becoming triggered, or highly emotional.

ABANDONMENT

I remember being shy and quiet as a child. I was also physically small. I received messages from a young age that children are to be seen and not heard. I did my best to stay out of the way or hidden; my small physical size helped. One of my earliest memories is of my mom leaving us. I remember my mother buttoning up my jacket, while telling me to be a good girl and take care of my sister. I am trying not to cry, but I feel scared. I silently plead with my eyes for her not to go. We call her parents Granny and Grandpa. They are not happy that Mom is leaving us with them. I feel like we are a burden to Granny and Grampa. They do not like us. I can tell, just by the way they look at us. Both Granny and Grampa glare and pinch and try to burn us with cigarettes. We try to stay outside and out of the way. They then tell us that we are a burden to them, and that our mother doesn't love us. I am four years old. My brother Brian is eight years old and my sister Samantha is three years old.

After a short period of time, Granny and Grampa drop us off at Lynn Bearheart's place. She is a distant relative. While staying at the Bearheart's, my siblings and I are remarkably close. There are other children at the Bearheart's, sometimes ten to fifteen children. The conditions that we live in are pathetic. The house has minimal furniture and is known to be the "party" house. Adults are coming in and out; there is a great deal of drinking and fighting. There is hardly ever any food to eat, so we are hungry all the time. The room we sleep in has no beds, only dirty laundry. At night we pile the laundry in a heap at night to sleep on.

My brother Brian liked to play pranks and do magic tricks. He was always creative at making up games for us to play. Sometimes we made bows and arrows. We didn't have any toys, but we had imagination. We envisioned so many scenarios, or rather, Brian did. I was happy to be the loyal sister waiting patiently for my turn. I loved my brother and looked up to him in so many ways. Sometimes Brian was mean, but I always forgave him. He was kinder than any other family member.

Samantha, my sister, was a year younger than me. She was bubbly and bright, and loved to be the centre of attention. Samantha would twirl, dance, or sing for anyone. Even though Samantha was sick much of the time with colds or ear infections, her need for affection and attention made her adorable and cute. During our time at the Bearheart's, Samantha's health was jeopardized by a lack of nutritious food and proper hygiene. Samantha was also deprived of any type of parental love. As Samantha's older sister, I did my best to take care of her as my mother asked, but I felt sad that I could not provide her with what she needed. Once when she was crying from hunger, I made us eat mud pies. She cried as we ate them. Most of the time, we tried to think up games to play to keep our minds occupied and take the focus off food.

Brian became adept at stealing food or money from the intoxicated people that looked after us. Brian also took produce from gardens and fruit from trees. Whenever he got the chance, he would grab and hide food for us. Brian kept us alive with this food, and we also learned to hide and ration food. Many times, when falling asleep hungry, we would talk and dream about all the food that we would one day have.

When the men were intoxicated, they came looking for the girls. I noticed that after each girl had returned, they would be hunched over in pain and crying. I was so young that I did not know what happened to them. One day a drunk man came into our room and he looked at me with blurry eyes. He told me to come with him. I was scared because I did not know what would happen, but I knew that I would get beat if I refused. I timidly got up to go.

My brother put his arm across me and said, "No, take me instead."

The man named Donald shrugs and said, "Ok."

Later, my brother comes back with bruises on his arms and face. He is different, he is quieter, he is not the same. Brian used to make the best games, but now he wants to be left alone. Sometimes Brian talks about killing Donald. Donald and his mother Lynn are our biggest tormentors.

Halloween comes and we can go trick or treating, even though we have no costumes. People still give us candy. We want to eat all our candy, but Brian tells us we should save some. He is right, so we ration our candy. As soon as Donald found out we had candy, he beat Brian up, punching and throwing him around. He is bloody and bruised before he gives in. Donald leaves and I know Brian is frustrated and angry. I wish I could do something, but I can't do anything. Donald uses our candy to lure the hungry girls to him. He then grabs them and touches them inappropriately. Brian tells me to never be lured by the candy and to keep Samantha away from Donald. After the candy incident, Brian hated him even more.

Brian said, "Samantha, You and I, should run away!"

Good idea! I'm scared, but I know together we will be ok. We make sure we have our jackets. Brian has a pillowcase with some stuff he has stolen for our journey. We must get over a fence and up a hill, it seems so huge. Samantha and I struggle. She does not want to go. She cries a couple of times, and we stop to hold her, and tell her we must go. It is chilly, cold, and dark. She wants the warm, dirty laundry we sleep on. We're scared to walk on the road, but Brian is convinced we have to get up this hill. I knew he could make it without us. I am grateful that he doesn't leave us. It takes a long time to make it up the hill. The stars shine so bright. Dogs bark in the distance.

Finally, we make it to the top. There is a wire type of fence at the top, we climb over that, and then Brian suggests that we rest." Samantha is cold and she is always sick from lack of food and milk. I try to warm her hands by rubbing them and placing them on my belly. We have some water and blankets in the pillowcase. We lay down and put Samantha in the centre to keep her warm. She is tired and dozes off. I have not heard Brian talk this much, not since before he took my place with Donald. It is so good to hear him happy. He talks about staying there forever. I am happy too. This is a good place, and I can stay here forever too. If I have my brother and sister. Everything will be fine. I doze off too. When we wake up, we realize we are in a graveyard. I am spooked at first, but then I feel relaxed when we get through the cemetery gate. Even though later that morning they caught us in a meadow. It was a special night and was worth the trouble we got into for running away. We were free, masters of our own destiny for one precious night. Together, we felt safe, like we could conquer the world!

In between this time, we were taken by social services and stayed at a foster home (the Tanners). I truly remember very little except that they were vegetarians and Caucasian. I was four. By this time, my mother and father have split up and I'm not sure where my mother was during this period of time.

DAD

I don't remember dad picking us up from the Tanners, but my next memory is of him taking us on a train. We are headed to Toronto where he has a job. Dad made us a bread bag full of bologna sandwiches for the trip. When he gives us a sandwich, it is so good! It tastes like love! When he tells us that we can eat as much as we like, we devour the rest of the bag like hungry animals. He is shocked that we are so hungry. Later he will tell funny stories of how we devoured the whole bag. The whole bag of sandwiches was supposed to last for the whole trip.

Toronto is so clean and has a lot of old buildings. My school is in an old building made of cement and stone. It is cold and damp. One day, not long after I started, I was sent to the basement to be punished. For what I don't know, but I am scared. I am told to hold out my hands and am given the strap. I am crying as I go home. When my Dad finds out, he goes to the school and tells them that if I am strapped again, he will have the school shut down. I remember feeling safe and loved. Never again did they strap me. We lived there for less than a year. Next, we moved back to New Glasgow to live in the old brown house.

DAD AND THE OLD BROWN HOUSE

I loved my father so much as a child, and I felt loved by him. My fondest memories of him are of living in the old brown house, where the gas station now sits.

Early in the morning I would wake up to him and Rose (my new stepmother) in the kitchen. He is happy. Breakfast is cooking. He is taking off to get gas. I pleaded with him to go too.

He said, "Are you dry?"

I pull up my pyjama pants and look down. "Yes," I reply.

"Good girl, ok then, grab your coat."

He swoops me up and we're off. I think I am around five at the time. While we drive, he cranks the radio and sings all the way. He loves to sing, and I think he is the greatest dad in the world. Chuck Berry (Johnny b Goode). He sparkles, and smiles. Laughing as I clap. I love him so much. I feel like the sun comes out when I get to spend time with him alone.

Dad gives us an allowance of five dollars each and we are so excited to have money. Times were tough for everyone on the Rez back then. One allowance day, he sits us down and tells us we can keep our allowance but, says that there is a family that is suffering, and they have no food. Dad is the chief, so he knows what is going on with families on the Rez. He lets us know that we can choose to keep our allowance, or we can choose to donate it to buy food for the hungry family. We have known starvation.

It is not a hard choice for me to make. I am happy others won't suffer from hunger pains tonight.

It is a sad day when we learned that dad lost custody of us in court. He took us out back to the woods and sat us down. He told us we were going to live with our mom. I did not want to. I wanted to stay with my dad. He told us we were going to go live with her, and we would not see him anymore.

I asked, "Could we visit," through tears and some pitiful whining.

He said, "It would be too painful to have to keep saying goodbye to us."

He explained that she would come the next day and that would be it. It was at that moment, that I had my heart broken for the first time.

MOM AND DAVE

The next day, we go to live with Mom and Dave. When we get to our mom's house, we learn that we have another brother, and his name is Eddie. He is good natured, and quick to laugh. I can love him instantly for he has a kindness to his demeanor. Always ready to share his toys, or time. He is maybe two or three at the time. I am seven, Samantha is six, Brian is eleven. For a time, we lived in Sidney in a duplex. Eventually we moved out to Ryan's Creek. It is a small town maybe a half an hour out of town. It is quite different from what we are used to, and there is a lot of racism.

One day when I am walking home, I see my brother walking and some boys are circling him making, mock native, "Woo woo woo!" sounds and spitting on him. I run towards him and call out. The boys laugh and walk away. In the beginning some kids could play with us. One girl had me over to her house one day and told me that she could play with me because, at least I was clean. I felt ashamed, and I kept myself neat and tidy from then on.

My mother was a mystery to me. I never knew what kind of mood she would be in when we got out of school. Sometimes she would be laughing and dancing around the kitchen, showing us how to do the twist. Other times she would be angry, banging and slamming things around as she cleaned. She was quite fanatical about the cleanliness of the house. After school we were to change out of school clothes and do our chores. She taught us how and they had to be done perfectly the way she showed us. One thing wrong like not wringing the rag out enough, or streaks on glass, warranted a slap upside the head. Eventually the slaps progressed into beatings and if we still were not smart enough, we were made to kneel on vents with a book on top of our head, arms outstretched as if flying. Try, doing that for even a half hour. It felt like torture. If our arms started to fall, she kept a broom stick close by to wack us with.

One day I came home to find her sick and lying on the couch. She asked me to go to the store to get her some soup. I did, only to find out the hard way it was the wrong kind. She whipped the can at me, and it dented as it bounced off my head, knocking me off my feet. She made me take it back, but would not tell me what kind to get. The store owner knew and felt sorry for me. He saw the dented can and the goose egg on my forehead. He asked me what kind I wanted. I tried chicken noodle. It took several attempts before she was tired of beating me and was so disgusted by my stupidity. Although she berated me for being so stupid, I was smart enough to know that I was not going to bring home any cans of soup ever again.

A Flash of light

The taste of blood in my mouth, blood
going to the back of my throat.

Another flash of light.

I can't make out what she is saying?

Smack! The sound is like a crack in my head.

Her open palm against my ear.

What is she saying?

"I Fucking hate you".

I see her face come into focus, as my wobbly legs straighten.

Why does she hate me?

BED WETTING

In the years of living in Ryan's Creek my life became hell on earth. By age eight my mother's violence was becoming increasingly brutal. In the morning I would be whipped until I trembled. I had a bed wetting problem. When I was younger, an older relative had tried to cure me by giving me ice cold baths. Then she would lock me in the bathroom. Making me sit on the toilet for an hour, with the lights turned out. She terrified me! My mother thought she could whip it out of me. She made me kneel in the centre of the bed with my wet sheet over my head as she whipped me with the buckle side of her belt. Later as an adult I would learn all these treatments originated at the residential schools. I stopped wearing shorts and t-shirts to school: and took to always wearing long sleeves and pants. It became common to be excused from gym class.

Although we were poor, and times were tough, Mom has some amazing gardening skills that helped to see us through. Dave, our new stepfather, also had a green thumb. Mom and Dave taught us how to grow a garden, and the garden was converted to an ice rink in the winter. Mom loved to can fruit and vegetables; she worked hard to prepare food for the winter. We always had a pantry full of food. Even though she said she hated me, and at times I believed it. She always made sure we had food. To me this proved that some part of her loved me. She made jams and syrups for pancakes. She made ketchup and canned jars of it, so we always had ketchup. Even Root-beer which we bottled and capped. She made a deal with the lady across the street to trade our vegetables for fresh eggs from her chickens. I remember being enormously proud of my moms' green thumb. We froze and canned a lot of food for winter. In the fall after the harvest, Mom would buy a truckload of manure for our garden. We would mix it in the garden, along with the compost pile we had made from eggshells and vegetable peelings. One year we had a surplus of manure, and she left a pile off to the side.

That year there was an article in the paper. Pumpkin growing contest. First prize, for age twelve and older, a new television. First prize for ages eight to eleven, a new bike. Mom gave us some pumpkin seeds. I planted my pumpkin seeds in the manure pile. Mom said manure helps plants grow, so I thought this will give my pumpkin the best chance.

My brother laughed at me and said, "it won't grow, it probably won't even sprout." I asked my mom.

She said, "I don't know."

I was determined. She told me that plants also liked to be talked to. So, every day I sat on the manure pile talking to my covered seed. Told it stories of my school days. Although my brother loved me, he found it difficult to be supportive (being the cool young man he was, athletic and all that). Anyways, you have never seen a kid so excited when it finally sprouted because by then, everyone's seeds had sprouted but mine, and I was losing faith that they would. But boy, oh boy once she started to grow, those seeds were like magic beans. I had a wild imagination back then, and thoughts of "Jack and the Beanstalk" played in my mind. Everyday after school, I sat talking to the plant first, then the actual pumpkin, and I swear the pumpkin loved it because she grew and grew like crazy! Everyone was blown away! The day before the contest Mom and Dave were saying we would need to borrow a truck and get some help to move that pumpkin. I was so proud. I just knew I was going to win that bike.

Brian had made both of us bikes constructed of assorted parts from the dump. He made his bike a lot nicer than mine, and he had spray painted his black, so it looked cool. Mine was orange, purple and black. Even though it was mis-shaped and multicoloured, I still rode it mostly by myself on back roads and after dark. Although I appreciated that he had made me one, I had to admit. I was embarrassed of the way it looked.

Just before we were ready to go my mom said she wanted to talk to me.

She said, "We need to give your pumpkin to your brother Brian, because we can win a new colour television in his age category."

I was a little disappointed but, at the time we had a black and white television. If my brother won (with my pumpkin) our new television would be colour. Everyone seemed to have a colour television except us.

She said, "Your big pumpkin is sure to win."

I agreed, feeling immensely proud to have accomplished something so big that it might win us a new television. Once there, my joy was deflated, someone came in with a bigger pumpkin and won the television. But because my brother's pumpkin was so big, he got to win a trophy with his name on it and his picture in the paper.

He walked past me running his hand over my face saying, "Poor Charlie Brown, even when you win you lose."

Mom never apologized, ever! I was just told to, "Watch out you don't trip on that fat lip."

I remember one of our favorite games was to pretend we were famous rock stars. We took a curtain down, (red crushed velvet), and used it as a costume, like an Elvis cape. We used a long dresser pushed to the middle of the room for a stage. Then we took turns on the stage with the cape singing along to some of Brian's L.P. records. Cheap Trick (I want you to want me) was Brian's favorite. I loved Elvis love songs, better cape action.

ALLERGIC TO BEE STINGS

One day when I was nine, I came home, and mom had been doing laundry in the kitchen. She asked me to change out of my school clothes. I put shorts on because it was hot, and I knew nobody from school would see me. Then she had a basket full of wet clothes that needed to be hung on the clothesline. I considered this the best job because you could enjoy the fresh air. I dragged the basket out and got to work when suddenly there were three bees, then six bees hovering around my head. One landed on my top lip. I stood very still watching it, too scared to try and swipe it away. The bee was vibrating and walking in a circle. I began to sweat from fear. Then he stung me. Oh my god that hurt! I ran off the porch to get away. The bees left me alone and went back into a crack in the roof, above the clothesline. I sat on the steps, at the far end of the porch, in pain, feeling my lip throbbing. Fighting back tears, I was too afraid to go into the house to tell my mom what had happened. I knew I would get a beating. My lip was also starting to swell in a way I had never seen before. Just then my brother walked up the driveway. When he saw me, he started to laugh?

"You look like a duck," he said.

I must admit that I could see my top lip and it had grown so big that I knew it looked like a duck bill too. I laughed and cried at the same time. Then he told me to go show mom.

I said, "No, she'll be mad."

He grabbed my wrist and started to pull me inside and told mom. Sure enough, her temper was lightning fast. She slapped me around the kitchen as many times as she could before I scrambled out.

She screamed, "Get those clothes hung! No excuses!"

Outside, I sat on the porch steps crying. I knew those bees would come and sting me again if I tried to hang the clothes. Besides, my lip was still getting bigger. It was like a balloon. Then I started to get lightheaded and dizzy. Everything started to go dark and drift far away. Then someone was lifting me up and screaming, but far away.........

I awoke in the hospital with doctors looking at my legs. I had changed into shorts after school. My bruises were showing. As I regained my senses, they told me I was allergic to bee stings and that I had been rushed to the hospital because my throat had swollen shut. I had stopped breathing, and Dave had come home from work just in the nick of time. He saved me. The doctors asked mom and Dave to step out while they asked me some questions. Although they moved out of the curtained off area, mom and Dave could still hear the questions. They asked me about the bruises and scratches on my arms and legs. I did not know what to say, I felt trapped.

The one doctor said, "Your mother said you fell down the stairs."

I said, "Yes, I did." I was too afraid to tell the truth. She was so angry, even though she tried to act polite to the doctors, and nurses. I could tell she was mad. I was scared that I was going to get it worse when we were alone.

DAVE

Dave was a tall white man with wavy light brown hair. He had bushy eyebrows and usually smelled like fresh cut wood. He worked at a mill as a foreman. Dave was kind and liked to teach us stuff: how to make shampoo, and conditioner from scratch to save money. How to make an ice rink. His mechanical abilities kept our second-hand station wagon on the road. On Sundays we packed up the station wagon and went to the dump to look for good stuff that people threw away, or bottles we could cash in. Then if we were good, they brought us to the lake for a swim and a picnic. He was very patient with us kids, and it seemed like he enjoyed our company. After dinner, the dishes were done. Mom and Dave would go relax in the living room. Mom usually lay on the couch. I would squeeze in wherever. Dave had his own lazy boy chair. If we looked squished on the couch, he would call me to sit on his lap. He said he liked it when I sat on his lap. He would talk nicely to me while stroking my hair and ask me how my day at school was. He would say my hair looked pretty that day. Sometimes I would fall asleep on his lap and he would carry me to my room and put me in bed and kiss my forehead. As my trust grew, I would fall asleep on his lap more and more. It became a regular thing to fall asleep there.

He began instructing me, "Go get a pillow and a blanket" before I sat on his lap. He would put the blanket over him, and I then he would tuck the pillow on the side (for comfort). He whispered little jokes in my ear, about whatever tv show we were watching. Sometimes when I giggled, he squeezed me tight to him like I made him happy. He had big hands, the right one he kept wrapped around me and the left one he rested on my thigh. Over the next few months, his left hand crept closer and closer to my private spot. Ever so lightly, he stroked my thigh.

I had no idea what was happening when the first tingles started to develop down there. Sometimes I would look over at my mom. He would say let your mother rest now she has had a hard day. Sometimes I would jump off and get away. If Samantha was close by, he would ask her to come sit on his lap. She always did. I had conflicting feelings about this. On the one hand I knew it was bad somehow and I did not want it, but on the other, I did not want it to happen to Samantha. Why did his hand make me tingly and dizzy? I tried not to think about it.

One time I tried to tell mom. Dave was watching me and put his finger to his mouth. He made a (shhhing) sound. I went to her room anyway. I blurted it out in a whisper because I knew he was close.

"Mom, Dave touches me down there." Silence, she said nothing. He came to the door.

She mumbled, "What are you doing in here?" I don't think she heard.

Dave was in the doorway. He said, "Time for bed, let your mother rest."

Later he progressed to coming in my room at night and touching me while I was sleeping. He never hurt me, only touched me, and licked my private parts. I was seven, or eight when it started. By age ten, I had figured out how wrong it was. I had also figured out that my mom had a drinking problem. She always had a stash somewhere. She also let me drink, although I hated the taste. Vodka, with water. I liked the numbing feeling it gave me. All my fears, and shitty feelings about myself seemed to fade away.

One weekend my Auntie Alice bought her family over for dinner. My cousin Mathew had a new bike that he took out to show off. I begged to have a spin on his bike.

He said, "You can go to the end of the block."

I am already half cut, and I have a mickey of Silent Sam vodka in my pocket. I am tired of being beat and told that I am good for nothing and being screamed and yelled at. She hates me, I know it. Deep down, I feel she knows what Dave does to me at night. I have a bottle of mom's pills. I'm pedaling and pedaling. There's the creek! I follow until I feel like my heart will explode. I jump off the bike and throw myself to the ground crying big racking sobs. I'm sorry God for what I'm about to do! I can't take it anymore. This pain is too great. I am so ashamed. I am weak. I take the pills and drink the rest of the vodka. The alcohol burns but it feels good. I just want to go to sleep and sleep forever. I am tired of all this pain. I wake up to Dave holding me. He is crying. I started crying too. Although I am semi-coherent, I try to push him away. "Please no, don't touch me". "I can't take it anymore". I am sobbing loud and hard. But I am too drunk to fight him off. He holds me tight. He is crying. "What am I doing to you?" Rocking me like a baby. I passed out again.

My Aunt Penelope comes to live with us, and she is fun. She laughs a lot and dances. Mom tells her it isn't right to be bouncing all over. She laughs it off. Dave likes her a lot, and I am happy about it because he is leaving me and Samantha alone, as far as I know. Mom is not happy about it which makes her drink more and be upset more. Eventually after a few months, Penelope and Dave run off together. I think that life is going to get better since he is gone. Sadly, it is not.

SUICIDE

Mom cries all the time and has taken to such depths of despair that she wants to kill herself. She has tried three times by taking pills. Each time I am there trying to console her. She is inconsolable. All I can do is call the ambulance each time.

I will share one episode with you.

I called 911, after she fell asleep, or passed out because she was drinking too. I was never allowed to call while she was awake. I would have to wait till she was out cold. I told the operator that she had taken the whole bottle of pills and that she had drunk a lot of Silent Sam vodka. They instructed me to scream, yell, and slap her while pouring water on her. Do whatever I could to keep her awake. My emotions where so mixed, I honestly believed that she stayed awake at night to figure out ways to torture me. I also believed that one of these days she would kill me, since the beatings were so severe. Anyways, now the nurse on the phone is saying to slap her. Oh my god, at first my slaps are not hard cause I'm still afraid of her. But then, I let my anger out and slap her harder, and harder, and harder, and still no response. Do I want her to die? Noooo, I know that no matter how much she hurt me she is my mother and I love her and want her to live. I keep hitting her but now I am crying. I try to drag her to the bathroom to throw water on her. Finally, I hear the ambulance sirens coming, adults coming. Thank god I do not have to be responsible for her life. I'm so tired but I must go find clothes for my sister and wake my brothers.

My brother's suicide attempts were much more mysterious to me. He hardly ever cried or talked about his problems. He just became incredibly quiet at times, then we would find him swinging by the neck in the basement, turning purple. One of the times we cut him down and he was still not getting air. I had found a little first aid booklet that gave crude instructions for a procedure to make a small incision into the neck and use a straw or small tube to put over the windpipe to allow him to get some air. My aunt Penelope was there, and we had assembled everything. Just as we were about to cut. We heard the sirens. The ambulance attendant came rushing in after I had swabbed his neck with the alcohol wipes. They stopped us and took over and made the incision. I saw the bubbles come through his neck.

Later, when the attendant asked me how we knew to cut his neck, I told him the little booklet had instructions. He was amazed that we were willing to try something so complicated. In my short life, Brian was the rock that I clung to, in the harsh world that I lived in. Even though I knew he didn't want to live, I needed him too. After my brother's 3rd suicide attempt, he went to live with Dad. I hoped he would be happier there because it terrified me when he became silent and tried to kill himself.

AUNTIE ALICE

My Auntie Alice came to visit us for a while. She had three children: Lexi, Mathew, and Vanessa. They thought we were odd, or rezzed out. We were afraid of everything and peeked around corners at them. They obviously had lived more worldly lives than us. They were much more confident than us, and it seemed they were never beaten. I thought they were amazing the way they held themselves bold with no fear and were able to talk back to their mother. My aunt had a lot of patience with her children, and as we got to know her, with us as well. I loved her very much. The oldest daughter Lexi could babysit us when Auntie Alice, and mom went out drinking. After a few months, their family moved on. I think my mom and Auntie Alice argued one night, then they left.

MOM MEETS KIRK

One night mom comes home with a guy named Kirk. I am 10, still small for my age. He sticks around for a couple of days. Then mom takes me, and him back to his place. They seem like they are in love, laughing and kissing a lot. When we get to his place they drink and take a bottle into the room. We are in a single wide trailer, which is very dirty. There is a very thin woman with long hair. She is sleeping on the sofa. Later I learned her name is Tara. After she wakes up, she is very skittish, and doesn't make eye contact. There are also 3 children there. They are watching cartoons. She prepares bowls of cereal for the kids and fixes one for me. I sit down at the tiny table to eat but there are bugs in the cereal, tiny black ones. I say to her, as politely as I can not to hurt her feelings that, ``I'm not hungry''. The other kids eat the cereal. Tara is cooking Kirk and my mom bacon and eggs. The trailer feels cramped as toys and clothes are everywhere. Tara brings two plates to the back room for my mom and Kirk. Suddenly I hear a commotion, dishes crashing. Then I hear slapping and hitting. Tara comes running, her hair flying. She runs behind me.

She is wailing "noo!!!! please noo!!".

He is taking off his belt. "Get away from the children," he screams. "Get over here now!". She bolts for the door and makes it outside.

He runs after her screaming, "You fucking bitch, I'm going to kill you!". He grabs a machete from the wood pile. He is chasing her in a rage and calling her all kinds of names. She shrieks every time he takes a swipe at her. I am stunned by the whole crazy scene. My mom comes out of the bedroom. All the children begin to cry as they are watching their parents. My fists are clenching, knots forming in my stomach. Why won't she run away? She is running in circles! It's the children. She keeps looking over to the children.

My mother screams, "Do something!" She grabs my arms, digging her nails into me. She shakes me. "Do something!"

I take a deep breath and walk out the door. He is chasing her around the yard. Luckily, there are things: tires, wood, car parts, and children's toys strewn about to give her things to jump behind. I walk towards them and come between them.

I put up my arms and say, "Please stop!"

He has stopped and is breathing hard from exertion. He still glares at her with anger and hatred in his eyes. He is dark skinned with shoulder length black wavy hair. He has a moustache and goatee. He wears skin-tight jeans and a tee-shirt with the sleeves ripped off. He is maybe 6' tall. I have learned in my short life to calm my breathing down when dealing with angry people. I am small so I must try to calm him. He is breathing heavy like he just ran a race.

He says, "You're not scared of me?"

He is so wrong. I am terrified, but I know that angry adults are like angry bears. You must not turn and run, or they will chase you. Neither should you look directly at them for that would be confrontational to them. Remain calm and only glance quickly at them. Keep glancing at the ground so that they know you are not challenging them.

I say to him, "You are scaring the children. You don't want to do this". I keep glancing over to the children's crying faces in the window. His eyes follow mine and I can see his demeanour change. He is calming and his breath, less ragged.

He asks me if I want to go for a walk. I look at my mom.

She motions for me to go. We walk off and he tells me about the Vietnam war. I must admit I wasn't listening all that well. Mostly, I am watching to see if he flares up into an angry rage again. The only part I remember of the conversation is that he has a head injury, and maybe that is why he gets so mad. The head injury gives him headaches. We are sitting on a bench and he seems to be in pain. He shows me the big scar on his head and asks me to touch it. I do and he shows some relief. He lies down on the bench and asks me to put my hand on his head. I do and he seems to be in less pain. He continues to talk but I can't remember what about. I just sit listening for a couple of hours till it's time to go back. He is smiling and laughing, and in a good mood when we return. I am careful to keep my demeanour neutral. I have learned the safest emotion to show is no emotion. Mom does not like to be at his trailer where his wife and kids are. It is too dirty for her comfort. I can tell, she is a neat freak. Thankfully, she doesn't complain because I know that he would take it out on Tara.

MOTORCYCLE

We return to the Ryan's Creek house. One day we are out driving. My mom drives the station wagon and Kirk drives his 350 Yamaha motorcycle. We are at a house with a long dirt road leading up to the house. There is loud music, and I am hanging around outside. There is a party going on. Kirk and mom are laughing and drinking with the people outside. I am looking at the bike. Kirk asks me if I want to go for a ride. I am excited, yes, I reply. I look to my mom to see her reaction. She just shrugs like it doesn't matter to her. Jeez I can't believe he is going to trust me with his bike. I know he loves his bike. He comes over and explains the throttle and brake. I get on but my feet barely touch the ground, just my tippy toes touch. He holds the bike up and tells me not to go too far down the driveway. Then tells me to jump on the kick start. I am not able to start it, so he starts it for me, then asks me if I'm ready. I rev the throttle and take off not too fast but fast enough so that I don't fall over. I'm off down the road. It is so exciting for me! Woooo! I get butterflies in my stomach! I keep going for quite a long way down the road. Eventually, I am out of sight or sound of the party behind me.

I start to wonder how I am going to turn around. I realize I will have to flip a u turn on the gravel road. I slow the bike down to make my turn, but I slow down too much and tip over. Darn it! The bike is on its side. I try to lift the bike, or push it off me, but it is too heavy. I am 4' 5" feet high, weighing maybe 80lbs. I struggle but can not get it up off me. My leg is trapped and every once and awhile, I try to push it off again. Thankfully, there is no traffic, so I decided to just wait. I'm sure someone will come, probably Kirk since I have his bike.

Sure enough, I see the station wagon coming. He jumps out and gets me out from under it.

I say, "I'm sorry." I am not sure how he will react, but he is not mad and seems to be more concerned about me, than his bike. I have a few scratches but nothing serious. He carries me to the station wagon. I'm sure I could have walked, so I am a little embarrassed.

This angers my mom, she says "she doesn't need to be carried".

He shoots her an angry glare. He sits me down and inspects my scratches and helps me gently to see if I can put weight on it. It is a little sore. I feel a slight pain, but nothing major. My mother has grown irritated at the whole situation. She is becoming more so by the minute. He asks me if I want to go riding with him when I feel better.

My mother complains, "why are you going to take her riding?"

He snaps at her, "You never want to go!" He has taken her out a couple of times, but she hates it and is very vocal about how much she hates it. They argue a bit.

Before we head home, Kirk is on his motorcycle, and me and mom are in the station wagon. On the way home he passes us and kicks the station wagon. This scares mom, and she stops yelling and being mad at him. She says, "He's f'ing crazy!"

KIRK VOWS TO PROTECT ME

The following week he arranges with mom to take me on a
bike ride. We will travel 4 hours on the bike. Lunch is packed
and his army canteen full of water. The day is warm and sunny,
but the back of the bike is windy. At first, I am trying to have as
minimal contact with him as I can, but after a while, he grabs my
hands and puts them around him and tells me I must hold on tight
and match his body when we are going around corners.

He says, ``We need to lean into a turn together.''

The helmet I wore did not have a shield and in the third
hour of riding I am trying to look around his body to see, when
something wacks my eye. I think it was a bee, or a beetle. Luckily,
I did not get stung. It got red and puffed up a bit but nothing
like the bee sting incident. We stopped at a lake and he cleaned
my eyes with some water and hugged me and said he was sorry. I
should have told him I was hurt. He noticed that I got hurt a lot,
because I always had bruises that I tried to hide. The lake is calm,
and bees are buzzing around. I'm not sure why the story of my
getting stung on the lip comes out but it does. I guess because I
didn't really know what to talk about with a grown man. Also, I
am a little terrified of bees and they are buzzing around.

He chased them away and then he lay back on his bike with
his hands clasped behind his head. He wore a denim shirt that he
opened to suntan, I suppose.

I walked along the lake shore skipping rocks, then looked

for pretty shells, or unusual tiny pebbles. He was wearing mirrored sunglasses, so I never knew if he had his eyes shut or not. Afterwards we ate our sandwiches and drank from the water canteen. He asked me how I felt, I told him I was a little shaky and was not feeling the greatest. He told me I would get used to it and that it was a long ride for my first time. On the way back he said he would stop more to give me a break. We had ridden for 4 hours straight. On the way back we stopped twice. I did not know what if anything I should say, so I kept quiet.

On our next stop he asks, "Do you like school?

"Not really." I reply.

"Why?", he asks.

"They don't really like me, and my mom lets me stay home to help her clean."

"What about gym or sports," he asked.

I looked at him and said, "Gym is the class I skip the most cause it's in the afternoon." "I can head home during lunch and avoid the changing room with the other girls." Mom writes me excuse letters for the gym, both her and I do not want any attention on my bruises. That would only make me more of a freak. Most of the girls do not want to associate with me already. I did not need to give them any more to talk about. Also, we have a new teacher. He is white with blonde hair, blue eyes. All the girls giggle and talk about how handsome he is. If he gives any of them attention, they become silly. I don't like him, I find him creepy.

One day I got detention for not finishing an assignment. He oversaw the detention room. When the others had all left, he approached my desk. I thought he was looking at my work because he asked if I needed help. He stood over me looking over my shoulder. I thought he was looking at my work, but he was looking down my blouse, When I looked up at him.

He smiled and said, "May I?"

I said nothing because I didn't know what he meant. He used his pen to pull my blouse out farther so that he could see my chest more fully. I was so embarrassed. My teacher then patted my back and said ok you can go. I rushed out and have avoided him ever since. Not sure why I shared that story with Kirk. I think I just felt alone and wanted to tell someone. Kirk seemed to care and called the guy a f"n a--hole.

He asked, "Do you want me to go beat him up?"

I replied "No, please don't. They will hate me even more." Tears welled in my eyes.

He said, "You can tell me anything." He kissed my forehead and hugged me.

"I will protect you," he said. I felt safe. As we rode back it was a lot chillier. My hands became like icicles. He took my hands and slipped them under his shirt, he said to keep them warm.

At the time, my only real friend was Lexi. She seemed so worldly, and confident. I felt like a little scared mouse compared to her. She was older by 5 years. She apologized to no-one. She smoked, drank, and told dirty jokes. She taught me to smoke, and not take myself so seriously. I idolized her. She was strong and quick to anger and fight if provoked. She looked like Joan Jet with the same tough attitude. She was Auntie Alice's oldest daughter, and I missed all their family when they moved on, but Lexi the most.

MY HAPPY PLACE

One day after the machete incident, I was out walking by myself: away from the dirty trailer, away from my angry intoxicated mother, away from the confusing situation in the trailer. My mother spent most of her time in the bedroom with Kirk. His wife, and I catering to them both. It was messed up, and at ten years old I knew that, but he kept her from beating me. Plus, she was not suicidal with him around. Anyways, I came across this field of green and purple and yellow. The day was beautiful like no other. I lay down in the lush green meadow. No one could see me. I felt so safe and protected.

I felt like I was having a special moment with the Creator. An indescribable feeling of love came over me. All my pain and shame floated away. I loved myself completely. As I lay there basking in the sun's rays, listening to the bird's chirp, colors became brighter and crisper somehow. This amazing feeling stayed with me for about an hour. As it faded, I got up and made my way back. That moment in time carried me through many dark days.

REPORT CARD DAY

After the first motorcycle ride, it became more common for him to take me along. On one ride while we were stopped Kirk asked, "What's wrong, I can tell somethings wrong?"

I told him it was report card day. I am afraid that I didn't pass. I knew I had skipped too much, even though my mom had excused a lot of the days. I had missed even more than she excused. Even today I was supposed to be in school. I felt horrible about it. School had become so painful. I felt so alone at school. The kids that did know me at school had seen the police and ambulances come to our house for my mom, and Brian's suicide attempts. I avoided talking to other kids because I didn't know how to answer the questions.

On the surface I could see that my family seemed to be strong. We were a tiny weak little raft in an ocean hurricane, ready to break apart at any moment. Mentally and emotionally, I admit I was so lost and confused that I had no idea what was going on inside anyone's head, even mine.

I explained, "It is report card day and I should be in school. I am feeling guilty. The teacher told us last week. The report cards would be given out today, and we would have to be there to get them." This deterred the children from leaving early to go on vacation with their families.

Kirk jumped up and hopped on the bike and said, "Get on."

I got on the back of the bike. "Where are we going?"

He said, "To get your report card."

I directed him to the door closest to my class. I could see my class was empty. All the classes were. They must have been at the school end assembly.

I jumped off the bike and said, "I'm going to try to run in and see if it's left in the class, but if not, we'll have to come back after school." I ran into the school.

He yells, "If you don't come back, I'm coming to find you!"

I know that no matter what, I will not keep him waiting. He has said he would love to bump into the teacher I had told him about and beat him up, but I am terrified of causing a scene at school. I tried so hard to be invisible at school! I run in the back door and the hallways are empty. I rush into my class and eureka! The desks all have report cards on them. A wave of relief washes over me. I snatch my report card and run back outside to hop on the back of the bike. I am so excited when we drive away. No more school, or even feeling guilty for not going and terrified when I do because I have no clue, and I am so far behind. The only thing I will miss is a girl named Danette. She was always kind to me. Although she was much taller, I never felt like she looked down on me. She tried to include me. I don't know if she knew how much I appreciated her kindness.

My happiness rubs off on Kirk by the way he rides. He drives in a wavy S like fashion. He takes us up into the mountains and to a lake. I jump off and I am so excited I am jumping up and down. This is so amazing! I feel like we were in a movie pulling off some big jewelry heist like the *pink panther.* Suddenly, I stop jumping and think, what if I fail and have to repeat the year? How humiliating!

I put my hands together and say a quick prayer, "Please God let me pass. I know I don't deserve it but please let me pass."

He says, "Open it! you won't know till you look."

I pass him the envelope, the report card is in it and ask him to open it, "I can't! Please can you do it."

He takes the report card and opens it, and after reading it for a second, he tells me that I passed.

Oh my God! I can't believe it. I am jumping for joy. He hugs me and I hug him back.

"Oh, thank you, thank you, thank you. I could never have gotten it without you." I know the school will call my mom in and she and I will go in to get it. But until that day comes, I am in denial and am waiting for judgment day. Before he lets me go from the hug, he kisses me, on the mouth! I try to get away, but he holds me tight. He watches me with his eyes open. I am shocked and do not know how to react, except to push and hit his chest. I am getting dizzy, and lightheaded.

Finally, he lets me go. He says he got so excited in the moment. I don't know how to act or what to say. So, I try to act like it didn't happen. He helped me get my report card. That was the important thing! I look at my report card. I can't believe they passed me. We laugh at the comments made about me and the air is light between us again. We return home to Mom and show her my report card. She cannot believe I passed either.

After that first kiss, he spends more time at our place. I can feel him watching me like Dave used to do, but it's different. When Dave watched me, I knew what was coming later that night. When Kirk watches me, I did not know what to expect and his gaze makes me feel lightheaded and dizzy, with knots in my stomach. When we are alone, he talks about how he is falling in love with me, and I do not know what to say. I don't know what love is, so I say nothing. One day he takes my hand and puts it on his bare chest over his heart and tells me his heart beats for me. I feel dizzy but safe and happy.

Over the next couple of months his attention towards me becomes more protective. He has the occasional outburst, and everyone goes quiet when he gets mad. Mom does not beat me when he is around. He has stuck up for me a couple of times, so she knows he doesn't approve of her beating me.

I was ten during this time and it was shameful for me to have these feelings at such a young age. I understand now that my hormones for sexual activity were activated early on by Dave. I listened to girls in school and I knew they did not, and we're not going through the same feelings as I was. I was deeply ashamed of my body and felt there was something wrong with me. At age ten I was very confused and said nothing because I didn't even have the vocabulary to define my feelings. I didn't have any supportive people in my life to share my secrets. In a week, I would turn eleven. It was a different time back then in 1978. The movie *Grease* had come out and was deemed too explicit for me to see. My older brother could go and see it. I remember how he teased me for being a baby and how the show was for grown ups. It was a different time to grow up in. I couldn't even imagine what the movie Grease would have in it. My brother Brian would sing the songs and make comments that referenced the movie, and my mom would scold him. I was confused and I didn't understand any of those jokes. I remember she hated him singing the *Grease Lightning* song. I didn't understand why?

BECOMING A WOMAN

My birthday is the following week. I am turning eleven. I do not remember what the clothes look like that I receive for my birthday gift. But what I do remember is the birthday card. On the cover it says 'So, you have a fat pussy.' And there is a picture of a fat cat on the cover. At the time I do not understand the sexual connotation of it, but I do remember being very embarrassed of the reference to me being fat. My mom laughs and thinks it's funny. I just get up and go outside. Kirk comes outside and tells me he does not think I'm fat.

I take long walks in the mountains by myself because I like to be alone and it helps me to stay in shape. Having missed so much gym class, I am self conscious about my weight. My mother punches me in the stomach when I walk by, telling me to suck in my fat gut often enough that I think it's normal. I am ashamed to say I started to treat my little sister the same way.

Now that I am eleven my mother says I am a woman and must wear a bra. Sometimes she makes me wear hers and I hate it. They have pointy tips and make my boobs look bigger because of the pointiness. She takes me to Sears clothing store to buy my first bra. I am so embarrassed. I do not welcome being a woman, in fact, I hate it. I do not like the way men look at my chest and stare at me. Sometimes I take some duct tape and tape down my chest. So many other girls want to have a bigger chest. Sometimes I see them put socks or oranges in the chest area to make their chest look bigger. I do not want what they want. It is an incredibly sad day for me.

I cry in the dressing room, "Please mom! I don't want a bra." She scolds me, "You put it on and get out here!"

I angrily put the stupid thing on over my t-shirt. I go out to the mirrors in the dressing room, where my mother stands with a sales lady. I am pouting and angry. My mother looks like she is going to get angry, but then she bursts into laughter. It is hard for me to stay mad. She laughs so rarely that it is like music to my ears. I realize how ridiculous I look and laugh too, still trying to hold onto my resistance to wearing this crazy contraption. My mom finishes her chuckle and tells me to get in there and take off my t-shirt. This whole turning into a woman thing sucks. At least my new bras aren't pointy.

THE MOUNTAIN

While talking to Kirk one day, I tell him there is a mountain I have always wanted to climb, at the top there is a cliff.

"I've always dreamt of what it would feel like to get to the top and look down."

He says, "I would love to climb that mountain and we should make a day of it. We can pack lunch." My mom has agreed to climb it also.

A couple of days later when the weather is good, we drive to the mountain. We decide which way is best to climb it. There is a ravine going up halfway, but it is a little steep for my mom. A little way away, there is a longer but easier ascent up the mountain, around the backside of it. I want to take the steeper incline because we have only so much daylight. I want to get to the top and back down before dark. I don't think my mom cares if she makes it to the top, but I do.

I ask my mom, "Do you mind if I take the steeper ravine way?"

She says, "Yeah sure, go ahead."

I work my way up and climb for probably three to four hours before I reach the top of the ravine. This is about halfway up the mountain. My mom and Kirk are taking the long way up the mountain. It's a beautiful day out, and the sun is shining. The rest of the hike will be much easier. I am going to make it to the top, and down in time!

Mom says, "If it starts to get dark and you're still not at the top, you have to turn around."

I agree. It takes me another two hours and I am just about to the top when Kirk comes up beside me.

"Oh, where is mom," I ask.

He says, "She turned back down. It was becoming too much."

I am not thrilled to see him. I miss my brothers and sister. My older brother is out of the hospital for another suicide attempt. But now he's gone to stay with Dad for a while. My sister is gone to stay with my Aunt on my mom's side to go fishing. My little brother is visiting our grandma on my mom's side. I am alone with my mom, and the night before, we drank vodka. After she got drunk, she took some pills, and talked about killing herself. These types of nights were rough because I feel so helpless. I am hungover and do not know it, only that I feel sad and hopeless. Halfway up the mountain I start to get nauseous. This ravine is steeper than I thought, and I am becoming frustrated. I might have to go back down the way my mom and Kirk were travelling. My thoughts are turning negative, fighting my way up. I think, why is everything so hard! I start to think of jumping off the edge of the cliff when I get to the top. So, him showing up just before I make it to the top is ruining my plan. I am so tired of this harsh life; I feel like giving up. I cannot see any future. I run ahead to the edge. I look over the edge, but I can't see the bottom. There is a ledge down there that blocks my view from looking straight down. If I jump I will only land on that ledge. Even killing myself is hard! Why can't anything be easy?! Tears are rolling down my face. The wind is coming up off the edge and whipping my hair around.

I hear Kirk say, "Even when you cry, you're beautiful." I try to smile but it is only a half smile. I am wearing a button up blouse. I become aware that he can see through my openings where the buttons are because my blouse is a loose fit white top. I try to close the gaps with my hand when suddenly he is in front of me.

He forces me to look him in his eyes and starts to kiss me. He is mumbling but I can not make out what he is saying. His mouth feels huge and again this dizzy feeling comes over me. He is unbuttoning my blouse and is kissing me all over my front chest and neck. I do not know how to act or what to think, everything is happening so fast. My body is tingling, and his body feels so hot against mine. I feel hot and cold at the same time. I am shivering and out of breath. He pulls me to the ground on top of him.

Once on the ground, he keeps kissing me all over and has my top fully open now. I'd had it tucked in, but it is all out now. He rolls me over so that he is on top now and he looks down at me. I am cold and scared but his actions are demanding but gentle. I think he may stop as he is looking down on me, I start to pull my blouse together. He has changed his mind and he is on top of me pulling my shirt open and kissing me again. He is squishing me. I cannot get air. He is rubbing his private part on mine and it's so hard it hurts. He is moaning and groaning now. I cannot breathe and I am only able to suck in air. Although this rubbing is hurting, I also have some tingling feelings that I can't understand or control. My body is shaking and convulsing. I still cannot take a breath. He shudders and goes limp. I am 4'5 he is 6' with a broad muscular chest. I am fighting to push him off because I can't breathe. He becomes aware and as he rolls off, I am gasping for air. I am shaking and trembling from the whole experience. Tears come to my eyes.

He grabs me and pulls me to his chest and says soothingly. "It's ok baby, I'm here. You are ok, you're ok, I wouldn't hurt you ever. I will never hurt you. I will never let anyone hurt you."

I am calming down and allowing myself to be soothed by his words, and the stroking of my hair. He pulls my chin up to look him in the eyes.

He says, "You are so beautiful." He kisses each eye and kisses my tears away. Then he pulls me into him and says, "Oh, what you do to me. I am weak around you". He shudders, and says he is drained and needs to rest a moment. I am regaining my composure too. I still don't know what to say, or how to act. So, I am quiet, still trying to understand these conflicting emotions. It feels good but also scary. So many intense feelings. Pleasure, but pain. Hot and cold. Soft, gentle, tender, intense, and demanding pushing. Like I was swept up in a tornado and set back down again.

He is concerned about my feelings now. "Are you ok? I am sorry if I hurt you! I lost control because you are so beautiful."

I replied, "Yes, and I couldn't breathe."

He looks disappointed, "But did any of it feel good?"

I suddenly feel shy and awkward, and put my head down and whisper, "Yes." He is thrilled and hugs me and swings me around.

He says, "I promise I won't ever hurt you again." I am happy he cares that he hurt me and promises to never hurt me again. He is kissing the top of my head and says, "Look at how messy we are."

He is picking sticks and leaves and dirt out of my hair, brushing off my clothes. After, he makes sure we are presentable. He takes my hand, and we start the long walk back down the hill. He is happy and along the way he sees a small tree. The tree is a little taller than him. He takes the tree and ties it into a knot. He says this is a love knot and that our love is sealed. The tree will grow like this with the knot in it.

He says, "He is mine now, and I am his." I am overwhelmed. No one has ever made me feel this loved before. No one has ever made me feel important, or special like Cinderella. Is this how Prince Charming and Cinderella are in private? I just turned 11 a month ago. I still think Prince Charming will come and sweep me off my feet. Could it be him? I don't know what to think. Only that it is always safer to keep quiet, and to say nothing.

DAVE COMPARED TO KIRK

The experience that happened with Dave had confused me so much and was so different from the experience with Kirk. I was seven, or eight when Dave started to molest me. It was never painful. He made sure to not squish me or hurt me. I had childhood fantasies of him saving me like Prince Charming, I was Cinderella. My mother was the wicked stepmother. However, that fantasy died, and I was a little crushed when he ran off with Penelope. I had just turned ten. Although, part of me was happy he left because I felt dirty and began to realize it was wrong. Also, I could see that he was making my mom crazy. Maybe she could become stronger without him? Maybe we didn't need him, and the dirty shameful things he did to me!? Even if sometimes they felt good, the shame that followed did not and was eating me inside. Dave never spoke or made any promises, only occasionally did he protect me from mom. I began to drink more of the vodka I found around the house. After Dave left, I realized he never really cared about me, or my mom. He just wanted his own sexual needs met, regardless of who he hurt.

Kirk said he loved me. When he tied the tree in a knot, it was a symbol of our love. The tree would grow, and our love with it. He said he would protect me; he would never let anyone hurt me. I had been hurt a lot and wanted protection and safety. My sexual hormones had already been activated by Dave. Although the sexual advances felt vastly different from Kirk to Dave. Dave made me feel like a child and he knew it was bad to want me. If I looked at Dave while he was touching me, he would take his hand and cover my eyes. It seemed like he did not want to see any questioning, or shame or sadness in my eyes. Somehow it was easier for him to enjoy what he was doing to me if he could pretend that I slept through it and did not know, or at least I could not see him.

Kirk wanted to be loved by me. He worked hard to get me to show him any kind of feelings I had for him. At first, I was scared and confused, thinking why does he want anything from me? He has my mom and Tara for that stuff? He was very vocal in his love for me and believed that I was special. He felt we were soul mates and destined to find each other. It was important to him that I was not afraid of him.

"From the first time you walked out in front of Tara, I knew you were special," he said. When he got these migraines from his head injury, he believed I could take them away, by putting my hands on the scar. He also made a point of having me touch him a lot: rub his back, hold him while riding; he took my hands and ran them up to his chest under his shirt. I had received very few hugs and kisses until he came along. Even compliments! He said I was beautiful, pretty, and special. I made him feel weak. He said he could barely control himself around me. Although it embarrassed me when he spoke this way, I got butterflies in my stomach. He was always looking for an excuse to touch me in public. I felt like I was falling in love with him, but I had no idea what that meant.

He asked me, "Do you think about me when I'm not here?"

When I said yes, he was over the moon. He picked me up and swung me around. I became giggly and laughed at how happy it made him. As his love for me grew, his impatience with my mother grew. He knew that she hit me and said that he hated it. He said I should be loved and cherished and that if he had the chance, he would sweep me off my feet, and never let anyone hurt me again! That sounded so romantic and heavenly to me.

My days of being beat so badly had reduced greatly since he was around.

Although he overpowered me in our make out sessions, he would stop if I said, "You're hurting me." He never penetrated me. If he tried to take my pants off or stick his hand in there. I panicked and tried to get away.

Then he would stop and say, "I'm sorry, I know you're not ready for that." He was happy to hold me and kiss me. He said it was getting harder for him to spend time with my mom. She drank a lot and took pills which made her irrational, and highly emotional. She became angry so easily, and I was the target of her anger. Most times he could deflect her anger away from me.

By this time, my brother was living with dad, and so was my sister. It was thought that my brother might do better with our Dad after his suicide attempts. My sister went because school was out for the summer, and she spent time between my aunt's, fishing, and Dad's place. Dad could never say no to her. I did not go fishing because I was allergic to bee stings, and the fish attracted bees in swarms. Although Eddie stayed home, he had friends close by the house that he spent a lot of time with.

THE SHELTER

I do not remember the fight between Mom and Kirk that leads us to being at the women's shelter, only that we are there at the women's shelter. My mom is sleeping. I am watching cartoons with my brother. One of the staff workers tells me that my father wants to talk to me on the phone.

I go to the phone and it is Kirk he says, "I'm sorry, I miss you."

I reply, "I don't think I am allowed to talk to you."

He says that he needs to see me to give me a letter for my mom. If she gets this letter it will explain everything. I tell him I can't get in trouble. He pleads with me and says he can fix everything if I will just come and get this letter. I hope he can fix things with my mom, because she does not hurt me when he is around. I give in. I am scared to go by myself and my little brother wants to come, so I let him. We leave the women's shelter and walk across the river to where Kirk lives about an hour and a half walk.

He says, "It would be better if we go talk up the hill for a bit." So, we go sit up on the side of a hill that overlooks his place.

I tell him, "I don't think the letter will work, but I will give it to her." Maybe she will forgive him.

He says, "What about you? Do you hate me?"

"No," I reply.

He says, "I just wanted to protect you, and I'm tired of watching her use you as a punching bag." I feel horrible and that this whole mess is my fault. I start to cry. Tara has approached us, and Kirk wants my brother to go with Tara back down to his trailer. My brother is four and he does not want to leave me. Kirk has a gun, but I don't think my brother, or I are in danger. I think my brother feels differently. My brother leaves back down the hill with Tara, but I can tell he is worried about leaving me. I keep reassuring him it's ok. I will be fine. The hill we are on turns into a mountain.

Kirk says, "I need more time to talk to you. Eddie will be more comfortable down at the trailer, Tara will make him a sandwich." After we are a little higher, we can see town, and his trailer. We sit down and talk. He tells me he only cares if I will be ok. I tell him that I'm fine and the shelter is ok. He holds my hand and kisses it and tells me he will go crazy if she hurts me. I keep trying to reassure him I'm fine and he doesn't have to worry about me. He says he can't help it. He's fallen in love with me. No-one has ever said they love me. He has said it a few times, each time he says it, tears spring in my eyes.

He kisses my eyes and tells me, "It's ok, you don't have to say anything. I know you can't love me the way I love you." I am confused. I do not know what love is.

RUNNING AWAY

We just sit there talking for a couple of hours before he brings up the subject of running away with him. I tell him I don't think I can. But he tells me my mom is going to be mad and will probably take it out on me for going to get the letter. I thought I could go get the letter and return before she woke up. It is a long time now and I am getting scared. I'm pretty sure she won't hurt me in front of the workers. But many times, when she wants to beat me and there are people around, she tells me to wait till we are alone. Then when we are alone, she thinks that I am taking advantage of having people around.

She says, "You think you're so smart and that you're not going to get it just because people are around."

Then I am punished even more severely because she had to wait to punish me. He is right, she will punish me. I am getting scared; I am in trouble and I don't know what to do.

He says, "We can run away. I will protect you. I won't let her hurt you." I must decide.

He says, "I will take you back if you want." I sit and cry hard for a while.

I tell him, "I will go with you. I can't go back." Maybe if I go, she will be sorry and never beat me again when I come back. I could not conceive that I would be gone longer than a couple of days to avoid her anger. Maybe things could turn out ok. We sit for a bit longer then we see police cars going to his place.

He says, "Your mom must have called the police."

I said, "What about my brother?"

He says, "They will take him back to your mom. We have a lot of climbing to do. Your brother is too little. He would not be able to keep up." Although my mother did beat my brother too, he had learned to be the jokester in the family and could make her laugh. Plus, he did not wet the bed, and wasn't a girl. That is why she hated me more. We started to climb and went deep into the mountains. The hiking kept me from worrying. I just kept putting one foot in front of the other. Deeper into the mountains and hills we went. Finally, we rested. He put his jacket around me while I slept on the hard ground, He did not try to be intimate with me.

We stayed in the mountains for a couple of days. In that time, he disappeared for a few hours leaving me alone. He came back with some warm clothes and a backpack full of food and a water canteen, sleeping bag radio, flashlight. I did not know what his plan was until just before we were to leave.

He said, "We are going to get on a train." There would be a train that night and after It got dark, we would be able to catch the train.

I asked, "Why can't we just take the bike?" For some reason I had thought that we would ride off like we had before and hang out by a lake for a few more days. My mom would miss me and be sorry. She would come to her senses and promise to never beat me again.

He said, "The train will be less conspicuous."

THE TRAIN

That night we came out of the woods and walked across a large field to get to the train station. I was surprised when he kept walking and we passed the station. We stayed in the dark until we were a dozen cars down. He found a box car with the door open slightly and hopped up. Then he took my wrist and pulled me up into the car. I thought we would be in the passenger car. I had ridden a passenger train with my dad. However, this was much louder and scarier. I had no idea where we were going, not sure if he knew either. It seemed like maybe he did. I was a little scared but when I would pause and start thinking, he would say something to reassure me we were doing the right thing.

Sometimes he just said, "You trust me right?" He had never hurt me; he had only tried to protect me and take care of me.

At this point in life, I had the impression my father did not want me. I rarely saw him, except when my mother went into the psychiatric ward. At those times he barely spoke to me. During the last visit when he was supposed to come to the house. I sat on the porch waiting all day. He never came or called to say he was not coming. As the day wore on, I felt my heart braking.

Even when I begged him, "Please dad, please let me come back! Mom hates me, she beats me!" He said nothing and acted like I had not told him.

I fell asleep on the train and awoke with the train rumbling to a stop.

Kirk said, "Wake up! We're getting off."

I said, "Ok," and got up.

We walk to town which is remarkably close to the train. He tells me to go clean up in the gas station bathroom. I do as he says and then we are getting back on the train. He bought us chips and pop. He also had sandwiches in the packsack that he brought. Kirk decides we are going to go in an engine car. This time there are four red engine cars lined up at the front.

He says, "They will only use the front one." He shows me how to get on the last one. Once inside he spreads out the sleeping bag. I sit down to have some pop and chips. I like this, it is much warmer and quieter. He is looking around at everything, there is even a water cooler with little Dixie cups. We drink some water. He also discovers a little trap door that leads to a bathroom.

He said, "It must work by burning up the waste and dropping them on the tracks." I used to love walking on the tracks, so I think it's gross! He settles down and stretches out on the sleeping bag. The train is taking a long time to start moving.

He says, "It's because it's so long." It creaks and shudders, then stops and does it again. I am sitting on the floor looking around when I start to smell this putrid smell like poo, or very dirty bathroom. I am looking around for what could be making this horrible smell. Kirk opens the trap door; he went into earlier. There are flames in the toilet bowl!

He says, "The toilet was full, so I flushed it". We grab Dixie cups of water and try to put it out. The stench is terrible, we open the door.

He says, "We have to go." We grab our stuff and go out the side and jump off. Thank goodness the train is not going fast. Once we are off, we run into the bushes. I feel bad that we didn't tell anyone.

He says, "They will see the smoke and figure it out." Sure, enough the train stops. They must be dealing with it. Ugh, that was gross! Some men are walking along the tracks to see if we are still around. We move deeper into the brush. The train starts to go again.

He says, "We will have to run because they are looking for us." They know someone is trying to hitch a ride. I do not think I can do it. It seems so high up especially the box car. He says, "We are going to hop on a grain car, and he points it out to me."

We get out and start running. He is behind me. He has explained that I am to use my right hand first because we are on the right side of the train. Once I grab on with my right, it is easy to grab the left and then my right foot then left foot. I think I might be too short, but I do it!

He hugs me and says, "You did it! I knew you could do it.!" The train has picked up speed. I have not thought about it before now, but I am a little sad. I didn't think we were going so far.

He asks me, "What's wrong?"

I tell him, "It seems like we are going so far."

He hugs me tighter and says, "We have no choice." He blames my mom and says, "If we get caught, we will be in big trouble." He loves me and does not want to see me hurt anymore. Even though my mom was mean I still love her, he assures me I will see her again.

He says, "Enough I don't want to talk about your mom." He changes the subject. After it gets dark, he tells me that we must sleep, so Kirk spreads the sleeping bag out.

He says," Take off your clothes." I am very shy; I leave my underwear on. He comes into the sleeping bag after me. I am so nervous; I don't know what to do. He lies beside me but propped up on his arm talking and laughing for a little while. Then he starts out by kissing and moving his hands all over me. Unclipping my bra and pulling off my underwear. Then he is on top of me trying to push it inside of me.

I cry and say, "It hurts." He tries to slow down and gets off me and lies beside me again. He talks about how he needs me.

I tell him, "I don't want to do this, it hurts. It feels like I am cut down there." He talks about how he sacrificed so much for me and that he loves me. If I love him this is what people in love do. I don't understand why because it hurts.

He says, "It only will hurt in the beginning." He pulls me on top of him and says there you have all the control now.

He says, "There now you're in charge," but I don't feel in charge. He positions his penis in front of my privates and says I can put it in slowly. He pokes it in just a little at the top. I can not bring myself to push myself onto it for I know it will be painful. He pushes me down on it a little more and I cry out again.

He says," Shhh Shhhh, it's ok, you're ok. It's ok baby, I love you. I would never hurt you." I try to squirm away, it does hurt. He lets me cry a little before he pushes himself up into me, and me down on him again. Then he does it again.

By the time he says, "look we are halfway, it's ok. You made it."

I go into full wracking sobs.

"You said it wouldn't hurt and it does! You are hurting me!" I pound on his chest. "I can't do this!" I am fighting hard to get away now. He grabs me and pulls my shoulders down and thrusts himself full into me. I feel a tearing pain down below and I let out a scream. I know nobody can hear me; the train horn lets out a long blast. He has his arms around my shoulder and is holding me in place so I can not hit him. I am crying in pain. He is saying there, there we did it. My face is drenched in tears. He is trying to kiss them away. After a few moments he starts to move his hips. Again, a burning pain down below.

I shake my head from side to side and say, "Please no, please don't."

He stops and says, "Ok, I will give you another minute." I wish I were stronger to fight and get away. I am trapped. Once I calm down a bit more, he starts again to move, groaning.

Again, I am begging him to not move, "Please, please, please." He is losing control and I don't think he can hear me anymore. He is moving all over. I am struggling to get away and I am crying. He digs his fingers into my arms.

"I hate this, please let me go, it hurts." It might as well be a knife down there.

Afterwards he holds me and tries to console me. Kissing away my tears he says he loves me, and it will get better. I will learn to enjoy it. I don't know how that's possible. I am angry and hurt but it feels good to cry in his arms and have him kiss away my tears. He has a red bandana that he gets wet and cools with the air. Then he applies it to my private area. The cool wet cloth eases the pain. I still cry myself to sleep. Maybe I made a mistake. What have I done? How often will I have to do this?

The next day he is on top of the world and so kind. The view from the rail car is amazing. We pass beautiful lakes. I sit and watch. He tries to set up the transistor radio, but only gets a channel for a little while. More static than anything. I try to imagine what my mom and Dad are doing, are they worried? Probably not. Mom is probably mad for sure. Dad is probably working; his work is especially important. I guess we will not be going back for a little longer than I thought.

He said, "We can't go back for a very long time." So maybe two weeks, rather than one? Best not to think about it. Although last night hurt and still hurts down there, I felt like he genuinely cared about trying not to hurt me? The sun was going down and were nearing somewhere that he wanted us to get off. I was happy about this because I did not know where we were. But, as we got further away, I was becoming more nervous. We got off the train and hopped onto another one.

He says, "We will wait till it is a little darker." He has friends here who can help. After the sun is almost down, we walk to the road, a paved highway. A truck comes and picks us up. I am sleepy and fall asleep in the back seat. He and the guy stay up and talk.

THE BARN

I wake up in a barn, it is dark. We are in the sleeping bag and he has taken off my clothes. He holds me and talks for awhile and then he gets aroused, and we repeat the previous nights sexual acts. It still hurts and I still cry. Later he soothes me and tells me I'm a good girl. He is sure it will get better; I must get used to it. I sob telling him that I don't think I can. He holds me and pats my back like a child, and I start to feel better after he comforts me. I like to be called a good girl; I've never been called a good girl.

After I stop crying, I ask him "Do you really think I'm good". My mother only called me down and beat it into me that it was my fault she hit me because I was so bad.

He says, "Yes, you are an incredibly good girl! I would not want to take you and protect you if you weren't." This gives me a happy feeling in my stomach, butterflies, I guess.

I wake up cold and shivering, but he is warm. I cover my head with the blankets till he wakes up. When he wakes, he tells me I have a new name. My new name is Rhonda Clairmont. I do not want a new name, but he says it is necessary. I am his younger sister, and I am supposed to be seventeen. I am not to look at the guy. He says he is very jealous and wants me to be only his. He also tells me the guy knows of our situation so that I should not try anything stupid around him. I don't know what that means so I say nothing and just nod. He said I will be babysitting two little girls in the trailer and he and the guy Donnie will be doing the farm work. I will cook, clean, and take care of the girls. He then takes me into the house and introduces me to Donnie and his two girls. The girls are maybe four and five. Their mother is passed on. I can tell Donnie loves his daughters and takes good care of them. The trailer is clean, the girl's room is clean. The girls are so sweet and listen so well. The first day, I am happy to be in a real home. It's warm and cozy. I was tired of always being outside. Also, it is nice to have real food instead of sandwiches and chips. I see there is a phone and think about trying to call my mom, but the thought scares me. Besides, I don't know any numbers by heart. The next day is the same. I think about using the phone, but chicken out.

WILD HORSES

One day on the farm Kirk and a few men are trying to catch wild horses. There are a bunch of wild horses in a valley and they want to catch a white and grey one. They believe it's the leader and if they catch him, the others will be easy to catch. Anyways, they bring me to a fenced in part, and I am supposed to push this big gate closed, when the white/grey one goes through. There are men on trucks and on horses. I am there for a while before they start corralling the horses towards me. I really don't want to catch the horses. They are so beautiful and free. They are running towards me.

I am whispering, "Please don't come here, it's a trap, runaway!" Please someone help me. I know these horses are happy and free. We should let them be. They are getting close, maybe 300 meters, and everyone is closing in around them to block their escape. They are not focused on me sitting still on the fence. Run away don't come this way! In my heart I don't want to trap these beautiful wild horses. Suddenly there were golf balls bouncing off the ground. The guys on the horses look startled. Everyone is yelling and pointing at me. I put my hand to my ear to signal I cannot hear.

"Whaaaat," I yell. Finally, the lead horse sees me, and changes direction. They are going to be safe. I am getting down off the fence, walking towards the truck. One of the golf balls hits my arm. Ow! It hurts! The guys on horses are making for cover under the trees while I'm walking towards the truck. They pull up and everyone in the truck seems concerned for me.

One of the guys says to me, "You could have been knocked unconscious if one of the hailstones hit your head!" The driver makes for a tree to park under. The windshield cracks where one of the golf ball sized hailstones hit. It is amazing! I am so happy we did not catch those horses, but I try to conceal my happiness. Although I am trapped, someday I will be free too. The weather is getting chillier in the barn. I think Donnie feels guilty. He tells Kirk we can sleep in the house.

Kirk said, "No it's ok. We are fine in the barn." I try to look like it's ok too. I am cold at night and my teeth chatter.

RUN PIGGY RUN

One day Donnie and Kirk are going to kill a pig and I am called out to help. I am supposed to throw the gate down to get him separated from the rest. I could not do it. The pig is running towards me squealing. I just can not do it. I can see the look of terror in the pig's eyes as he screams for help!

Kirk screams and yells at me. "What the F--K is wrong with you? You f---ing lazy cunt. You don't have to do anything around here. I do everything for you, and you don't even deserve it."

I cry saying, "I'm sorry." I start to run because I know he will beat me. His anger at me has been getting fiercer. He flies into violent rages more often. I wake up to him choking me, and a crazed look in his eyes. If I cry at night because I want to go home, he will start punching me in the stomach knocking the wind out of me. The man gets between us and tells Kirk to calm down, there is no time for this. I am safe for the moment. They end up trapping and killing the pig. I only spare his life for a short time. I cannot eat pork or bacon for a long time. Kirk makes me come outside and look at the pig. It is hanging and they are burning the hair off it. The smell is disgusting. Afterwards they go to town and drink, they come back half snapped. The next part is fuzzy. I thought the guy knew about me, but Kirk gets mad when the guy starts asking questions. He knows Kirk beats me. I think he questioned our relationship? I know I have considered calling home when I am alone. I am tired of this life and I want to go home. I think we have been here for a month, maybe?

WINNIPEG

We are in a house. The house is shabby, old, and dirty. I believe we are in a city. There are houses around us. Kirk has a truck. I don't like him anymore; he is mean and awful. I thought he would be kinder to me than my mother, but he is worse. I want to go home. This is a bad mistake. He must let me go. I hate him. He just wants sex, and gets mad if I cry, or say it hurts.

He calls me names, "Slut, dirty whore, cunt, bitch. You are nothing without me! Nobody cares about you." I realize I am so stupid. I did not look ahead. I am such an idiot. I deserve what I get. He wants me to grovel, or say I love him, or some stupid shit like that, but I despise him. He disgusts me. He is so controlling that he won't even let me go to the bathroom with the door shut. He portions my food. He makes me do exercises for two hours every day because he does not want me to get fat. He bathes me like a child every day, after he pours cold water on my privates. He said this will keep the skin-tight. He spoke about how he gets migraines and likes me to put my hands on his head. He believes it takes away the pain. I don't even want to take the pain away. He said the scar on his head is from the Vietnam war. He also likes me to rub his back. Many nights I wake up to him choking me with a wild look in his eyes. I'm quite sure he can't see me, just as I'm blacking out. He lets go and cries while he apologizes. He makes me hold him. I can't help but feel a little sorry for whatever must have happened to him. Still, I want to go home. After I would have sex with him, I would try to get dressed, but he would not let me. Sometimes I could wear a nightgown.

He says, "You belong to me! This peach is mine." As he grabs my private parts, squeezing hard. Then he grabs my breast and says, "If I want to look at them, I can." I am starting to hate not having any control over my body. I am now sure I must get away somehow.

I do not remember the events leading up to my escape, but only that I made it out of the house. I am running and running down a back alley. I keep looking behind me. My heart is racing so fast, I'm almost free. Just keep going I tell myself! It is dark out. Oh my God, he is in front of me. I don't know how that happened. I am terrified.

He grabs me saying, "After all I've done for you! Don't you know that I've fixed it so you can never leave me! I put Indian medicine on you!" He did something with my shoelaces, and a lizard. He says that the tree he tied was also to hold some love spell, or something like that. "You, can never leave me. The only way you will ever get away from me is in a body bag." I'm done.

I whimper," Please, I'm sorry I'll never try to leave again." Even as I say it, I know it is useless. I will get the beating of my life. Sure, enough he starts punching me in the head as soon as we get in the house. I see flashes of light when the blows connect. He slaps and kicks me downstairs to the basement. When I hit the bottom, I can't get up. This angers him even more. Then he is punching and slapping me, finally he rapes me. I am a bloody swollen mess. My whole body hurts. He is sleeping on the floor beside me. The floor has an old red short hair carpet. When he wakes up, he feels bad about my face.

He says, "Oh boy why? Why did you make me beat you?" Tears well up in my eyes and roll down my face, which hurts more now from the cuts exposed to salty tears.

BREAKING POINT

He comes over and starts to kiss my tears away "sh, sh, there, there. That's a good girl". He takes my arms and wraps them around his neck. I try to choke back sobs, as he rapes me again. I try to let my tears stay blurred up in my eyes, so his face is a blur, because I don't want to look at his face.

After he is gruff and tells me, "Get upstairs and make me something to eat." I try to put on a nightie he bought me, but he grabs it and yells, "No! clothes are a privilege, and you lost the privilege to wear clothes!"

I can do nothing but obey. Not sure how many days and nights pass. I am locked in a small room in the basement still with no clothes. I am only allowed to go up to cook him something. He is picky about how I cook or clean. If I do something wrong, I get beat. Sometimes, he goes off for no reason. I am losing hope. How much longer can I last? Sometimes he lets me listen to the radio, only to tell me see, no one is looking for you. He talks about another girl he took before me, how she's the true love of his life. I don't care, I hate him, but I cannot say that. Sometimes I roll my eyes in disgust, but never to his face.

Once he caught me, I was beaten and forced to miss a couple of meals. I no longer cared if I ate. That was not allowed either. If he noticed I stopped eating he would force feed me and beat me. One day I came across a package of Contact C. I cannot remember exactly how many were in the package. I think it was eight or nine. I snuck them downstairs and hid them in the closet. When he would lock me in, he would give me a bottle of water, and a bucket to do my business in. I do not know where he went, but I know he would sometimes pretend to leave to try to trick me. If he heard me trying to get out in any way he would come in and choke me. Anyways I had the pills and decided if that is the only way to get away then so be it. After he left the next day. I took all the pills and prayed please god let this be enough. It was not, I awoke to him kicking me with his cowboy boots on. I was getting kicked all over and he was screaming, but I was so tired, and was hurt! I couldn't understand what he was saying. One of his kicks connected with my ribs, suddenly I could not breathe. I was sucking in but could not breathe out. By then I had stopped protecting my face, I saw his boot coming straight for my face. Darkness fell, and I welcomed it.

I wake up, I am hanging by my wrists, it hurts. He has me tied to a pipe in the ceiling and if I stand on my tippy toes it relieves the pressure on my wrists. He has masking tape, and he is putting the tape around me, on my ribs.

He said, "You have a cracked rib and that's why you can't breathe."

He goes on to say. "I should have just let you die. Nobody cares about you anyways. I would have been doing the world a favour. You're pathetic!" I feel I am. I cannot even die. He's right I can't even kill myself. I feel I'm close to death anyways. I decide to just let it all out and maybe he will beat me to death.

I tell him, "You're a sick monster I could never love you! I hate you. I wish you were dead!" I spit at him, and said, "You disgust me." It's working, he's flying into a rage I can see it. He starts hitting me, then cuts me down. I cannot move, he slaps me a few times. He rapes me and chokes me at the same time.

He said, "Say you like it you little cunt, say you love me you bitch, and I might let you live." He chokes me and I pass out again. I come to, he is slapping me

"Say it, you f---ing bitch, or I'll kill you!"

I say," Go ahead do it, do it! I hate you! how could I ever love you? look what you've done to me!" He chokes me again.

As he is choking me, he says, "I'm going to leave you here to die, a slow death, maybe I'll come back, maybe I won't? But you better fucking believe if I do come back! I will not take any more goddamn shit from you. Maybe I'll go find that little sister of yours. I'll bet she's not a little cunt like you. If I give you one more chance to love me, you goddamned better appreciate all I have done and sacrificed for you! If, and that is if, I come back, you better convince me that you love me, and you need me, or I will leave you here to die. I can find 10 bitches like you." I have played my last card. He leaves me in the dark. I let myself drift off, maybe I won't wake up. I do wake up, barely. I don't know when my last meal was, or sip of water. My whole body aches. I try to get up, but I cannot. Each breath brings a sharp pain. My face is all bloody and swollen. I can barely see; my eyes are almost completely shut. I just lie there feeling so vulnerable, still naked. I imagine the police finding me like this and I wish I had clothes on. I try to roll over, but I cannot. I am awake for a few hours, wondering how long I have been here. Is he coming back? I am so thirsty. I try to pant to ease the pain. Finally, darkness comes again. I fall asleep. When I wake, I wonder what my family is doing? I remember him saying something about taking my sister. I try to scream, but I cannot. I am so angry. I hate him so much. I cannot protect my sister. I try to cry out for help. There is a sharp pain in my side. My voice is raspy, and I know no one can hear me. I try to turn over again. It takes me hours of effort and a lot of pain. I figure if I can roll over. Maybe I will be able to stand. If I can stand, maybe I can somehow shatter the small window. I have always been too scared, but he is gone. It's been at least two days, by the sun and dark. I spend the whole next day trying to summon the strength to get up. I cannot, I have many conversations, mostly in my mind. My throat and lips are becoming so dry that I can barely get saliva. I had thought I would be able to get up. There are certain positions that make it easier to breathe. I try to crawl towards the window thinking if anyone comes around and I am directly under the window, they might see me, or I might find a burst of energy to yell. I barely make it a ruler stick length to the window. I keep passing out. I now realize I am dying a slow death. I am so thirsty. I can sleep more and more. I am becoming scared. I hate this ugly basement; I hate all basements. They conjure up images of my brother hanging. I do not want to die in this disgusting basement. I pass out again and wake up in the dark. Am I dead? No, I hurt so bad and the thirst comes back. I feel so heavy, and I cannot lift my head. I let myself fall back asleep. I hear a noise and I wake up. I try to yell for help. It is a strange sound that comes out of my mouth. I try to open my eyes, but I can't. They are glued shut. My tongue feels thicker, like it is three times the normal size.

In my darkest hour, I made up my mind. I wanted to live. I told myself If he comes back for me, I will be good. I promise I will love him, and I will never try to leave him again. I chanted these things over and over in my mind as I slipped in and out of consciousness. I think I am on the floor for four maybe five days, before I see him again. Maybe he is here there the whole time, but I do not think so. A few days later he appears. He must have had to nurse me back to health somewhat because I know I have lost the ability to speak or move. Sometime later, I awake, and I have a blanket covering me. Kirk is holding me. He places my arms around his neck. I am crying. I can barely talk, but I am trying. He must have already given me water. I am trying to tell him I've missed him so much and please, please never leave me again. He can not understand me. My tongue is swollen, but my tears, and the way I am hugging him lets him know. He is kissing me, and makes love to me, explaining that making love is different than fucking. I do the things he wants and likes, no holding back. I can not live without him. I love him and I will do my best from now on.

He whispered to me, "Shush my sweet baby, are you going to be a good girl?" I nodded as fast as I could. I let go of my ego and my stubborn will. The only will I had left was the will to live, I will survive. He loves me, even though I cause him so many problems.

At night he said he needs me. He sleeps with his arms and legs covering me. There is a bucket for me to pee in when he doesn't trust me. When he trusts me more, I can use the bathroom, but the door must stay open. I try to be good now. I'm tired of his wrath. I try to learn how he likes everything. I can tell that he has nightmares because he sometimes yells and thrashes around. Sometimes he starts hitting and choking me. I fight him and he wakes up. Then he cries in my arms.

I hold him and whisper that It's ok, I'm right here I will never leave you. He never says what he dreams of. The look on his face is of pure terror. His eyes bulge out. I don't really want to know anyways.

My next memory is of him telling me that his wife is coming, I am scared. Maybe she will hate me. I do not know what to think. He thinks I am jealous, and he buys me a lacy pink nightgown.

I tell him, "I love it."

He tells me, "You will always be my special girl. I am risking my freedom for you." I hug him and kiss him. I no longer fight with him. I try to make him happy.

TARA

When Tara arrives, she has the three children with her. Tara and I are both shy with each other. We both try to smile in front of Kirk. He lays out all the rules. I am to help with the kids. I don't mind because I like kids. We both will cook, clean and we will all sleep in the same bed with him in the middle. The first night he makes love to me first, then later in the night, he makes love to Tara. I turn away and pretend not to know. The next night he makes love to me but pulls Tara over and kisses and fondles her as he is on top of me.

Then he switches to her and tells me to rub his back and body. I am uncomfortable and shy, but I do as I'm told. The next time he tries to take it further. He wants me to touch her. I touch her back and breasts but start to cry when he tries to get me to touch her down below.

I whisper, "I can't, I won't." He tries many ways to show me what to do, but I pull away. I can't. Thankfully, he doesn't push too much for that. At a different time, he encourages her to touch me, I'm ok with the top, but when he gets her to go lower, I do my best to squeeze my eyes shut, and clamp my mouth shut.

Tara says, "Please don't make me. She doesn't want to either." Tears are coming out of my eyes.

He wraps his arm around my head, and says, "Awe, my baby is crying." He kisses away my tears, and I let my tears gush from the tenderness in his voice. He says," My sweet baby girl. It's ok.

Are you crying because you don't want anyone else to touch my peach?" He cups me down there. I am blubbering now, but I nod my head up and down. He said this is my peach, and nobody else gets to touch it. He squeezes it and tells me to say it.

I sob out the words, "This is your peach, and nobody but you can touch it." This arouses him and suddenly he is devouring me. I allow myself to be swept away in his desire for me. He loves me, he does not want anyone else at this moment. I am not alone. If I am good, he will not hurt me, and he will protect me.

BECOMING FRIENDS WITH TARA

Becoming friends with Tara was easy. It was hard not to like her. In the beginning I sensed that she was as scared of me as I was of her. I felt that she wanted my friendship as much as I wanted hers. She loved her kids and doted on them the best she could. Kirk got a job which meant Tara and I had time to get to know each other. He didn't like us talking too much when he was around. We loved talking and joking around when he was not there. She had a great sense of humor, and a great laugh. Things were much more comfortable for both of us when he was out. When he was home, we were both on edge and kept our heads down. His temper was lightning quick. I could get smacked or hit with something before I even realized he was mad. One time I woke up on the living room floor, with blood on my head. I had no idea how long I had been knocked unconscious. When I tried to get up, I was too dizzy. I slumped on the couch. Later when Kirk left, Tara brought me a cool, wet cloth to clean the blood off. Although he was cruel and vicious to me, I don't remember ever being degraded in the same way as Tara. He would get her to pull down her pants, even in front of the kids, and strap her with the belt like a child, only much harder. Even though I tried to make the best of the situation, I still fell into despair at times. The only time he was kind or nice to me was when he wanted me sexually. The rest of the time he called me down and belittled me. Kirk constantly told me that no one cared about me and no one was looking for me. Without him I would become a whore on the streets, like the last girl he took before me. Kara was her name.

After a few months, my depression was getting the best of me. I gave up because he was never happy with me. No matter how hard I tried to be good, he hated me. He resented me for losing his freedom. I stopped eating, I just decided to starve myself. When he realized this, he tried to force the food into my mouth, but I still would not eat. Even though I got punched in the head and hit at every meal, I still would not eat. I found my ticket out, even if it was to be in a body bag. I tried talking Tara into helping me escape, but she was too scared. I think I was too, but when I went on the hunger strike. I felt some power return to me. This made it easy to fight through the hunger pains.

One night he got mad, and said, "No wonder you won't eat. This food is shit." He picked up the table and flipped it over. He punched me in the face screaming, "You fucking bitch, you think you can beat me." He pulled off his belt and started strapping me all over. I shrieked in pain. He kicked me to the floor screaming and told me to eat the fucking food! There was food all over the floor. I crouched on the floor, but I would not eat. If he beat me to death, so be it. I was ready. Then he called Tara in. Her and the kids had taken off to the living room to stay out of harm's way. I could tell she was scared. She was always scared, but sometimes she shook harder than others. She inched her way in. He motioned for her to get on the floor and told her to strip. Then she really started to shake. I was still crouched on the floor, amongst plates, food, and the table. Now I became scared and jumped when he barked at her. Usually, he would make her pull her pants down, and bend over, and position herself in an improper push up, with her bum raised. This time he wanted her to strip naked. My heart started to race, please no.

She is shaking so bad, but she does what he says, and strips and gets into position. He starts to hit her, the sounds are horrible, as the strap wraps all around her naked body. She is trembling from the pain. I see welts form on her. Oh my god this is my fault. He probably hits her maybe five times as hard as he can.

I cry out, "I'm sorry please stop." I start to grab food off the floor and eat whatever I grab. I am sobbing, "Please, please. I am eating. I am eating!"

He is whooping her so hard! He turns the belt around and is beating her with the buckle. Bloody welts are forming. She can't stay up like that. She falls to the floor.

He is screaming at her, "I told you to keep her in line." He means me. Over the last week she has pleaded with me to eat. I'm so sorry. She is just lying there unconscious. He beat her till he is exhausted. Then he gives her a good kick, as he leaves.

He says to me, "Clean this fucking mess." I go to her. The kids are all watching and crying. I tell them to go watch TV, and that I will take care of their mommy. I help her to the bed and tend to her wounds. She is shaking from pain, not fear. I am ashamed that I put her through this. I will try to be better. I will be good. I cry as I clean up. There will be no escape.

THE ESCAPE

Over the next couple of weeks, she seems changed. Her little boy starts hitting her, and we talk when Kirk is gone. She can see, as much as I can, that her children are witnessing her abuse. This is affecting them mentally and she is concerned. Together we start to hatch a plan to run away. He keeps the keys on him. She wants to take the children. I can see she is terrified and so am I. Her children give her courage. She sees they will become abusive, or victims and she doesn't want that for her kids. He has a big scar on the backside of his head. I will hit him on that spot. She will gather the kids. Once he goes down, I will go through his pockets, and grab the keys. We will put the kids in the truck. I will drive us out. I have watched and tried to memorize what he does, anytime he has let me out in the truck. I drove my mom's station wagon once. I must believe I can do it or else. There is no option, she will not leave the kids. I cannot leave them. I am so scared to hit him. I've decided to use a two by four. This is what he hit me with before when I was knocked unconscious. I am scared to kill him, but I need to hit him hard enough so that he is immobilized, preferably knocked out.

The moment arrives. I do it, I aim for the spot where the scar is. I'm so scared, but I do it. Whack! He goes down. I drop the two by four and start to rummage through his pockets. He is moaning. Oh my god. He is not totally knocked out. I yell at Tara to hurry and that we gotta get out of here before he wakes up. We all pile into the truck. I have the keys; the truck turns over. Yaaa! I put my foot on the clutch like I've seen him do... I try to shift it into gear and the truck lurches forward. It slams into the house and dies. I am shocked. It is only a minute before Kirk comes out of the door and rips open the door. He grabs me by the hair and pulls me out. I am dragged into the house by my hair. Pain, Pain, Pain, Pain, Pain, Pain, so much pain. Please god help me, take the pain. Take me away. Why? Why, please let me go!

We both get a dreadful beating and are separated. I am put back in the basement. He knows it was my idea. It will take me several months to earn his trust, to get my clothes back and get out of the basement.

A JOB

I have been good for several months and he is beginning to trust me again. It's been over a year since he has taken me. He wants me to get a job. A job, oh my god, I have never had a job before. I am so excited, what if the boss does not like me? What if I don't get the job?

Kirk says "If you don't get the job, you'll be sorry when we get home. You need to start pulling your own weight. I'm sick and tired of paying for everything for you ungrateful bitches." I am so excited. I hate staying home and cleaning. We can never discipline the kids or try to teach them anything. It's just running behind them cleaning, as they mess the house up. If we try to discipline, Kirk gets mad. The house is always dirty. I want this job so bad. Kirk has taken me to his workplace, and I have helped him when no one is around, he showed me how everything was done. Please let the boss like me and hire me.

The job site is in a warehouse, Kirk, and another man who is Inuit, are the only workers. The other man's name is hard to pronounce, so they call him Lance. Lance is incredibly quiet and keeps to himself. From what I can see, he is a hard worker. At the warehouse they cut stone for fireplaces and fancy walls. The stone is quartz and has a little bit of sparkle in it. I love the way it looks when it is wet. The boss's name is Gabriel, but everyone that I hear calls him Boss. I am so nervous when I climb the stairs to his office. He is nice, with kind eyes. Kirk has coached me and

72

told me that I better not go in there acting like some scared little mouse! I try to put my shoulders back and look him straight in the eyes, even though I am very scared. Maybe he'll know I'm lying about my age, or who I am. Please Creator, I need this job.

I realize as he is telling me he will think about it, he is not impressed. I've never had a job before, and if I am 17 and a half like I told him, I am small. He is dismissing me. I pluck up all my courage and walk up to his desk.

I tell him, "I know I'm small for my age, but if you'll just give me a chance to prove myself, I swear I will work harder than anyone here. I will start before everyone and I won't stop till everyone else has stopped." There are only two workers. He is shaking his head and looks at some papers on his desk.

I tell him, "I'm a fast learner. I will work for free for one week, and at the end of the week, if I can't do the same work as anyone else and keep up, I swear I will just leave quietly. Please sir, I swear, you will not be disappointed. I will do all the clean-up first, then when I'm done, I'll ask the guys to show me the harder jobs to do, like operating the saw. I really need this job, please Sir." He finally agrees. I am so happy. Later at home Kirk is mad that I am working for free for a week. I am not. The week will fly by. It flies by and true to my word I work harder than anyone else.

All I care about is work. I do not feel the pain in my hands from being cut up by the stone. I work 16 hours a day. When I'm tired, Kirk will put me on some cardboard boxes and raise me up on the forklift at the top of some shelves high up. It is warmer and quiet up there. I can sleep for a couple of hours till it's time to work again. All I want to do is work. I hate going home. At work he is nice to me. For the most part, Kirk keeps his anger in check unless nobody is there. For the first time in my life I feel valuable and important. I must hide these feelings. It makes Kirk so mad if he thinks I'm happy and he's not responsible for it. He hates that the boss smiles at me and is kind to me. I try to remain stoic and not show how proud I feel of this accomplishment. For the first time in my life, I am not a failure.

Except one day I fall asleep standing up operating the table saw. I am so tired. Luckily, Lance is close by. He pushes me, just before my face is cut. I have learned to sleep standing up. Quick cat naps that refresh me when the hours are long. I prop myself up in a corner for ten minutes, that is all I need. I do more pallets than anyone else, including Kirk. Most times we work eight to twelve hours. Sometimes, the boss says he has a rush order to do. If we want, we can stay if we need to get it done in time. I would stay sixteen hours every day if I could.

I never saw my pay. I have no idea what or how much Kirk made from my work. Although he never said it, I knew I made his life easier for a bit. Calling me a lazy, stupid, dumb, good for nothing cunt, rolled off of my back. As well, as telling me how much he sacrificed for me, and I didn't deserve his good treatment, did not stick to me like before. All I wanted to do was work and stay out of his way. I did not think of anything when I worked. I just focused on doing everything perfect. He even started leaving me at work by myself at times. All I thought about was cutting the next rock, keep cutting until you fill a box and keep cutting until enough boxes fill a pallet. Clean your area, wrap your pallet with plastic, and then metal bindings. Use the forklift to move the pallet to the shelf for pick up. Start over and stop only when necessary. Food, drink, bathroom, and sleep. It was a never- ending safe loop. I found a quiet safe place in my mind. I gave in to the idea that this was my life now. I no longer expect, nor wish for more than I had, I was safe. I did not allow myself to want or ask for anything. I allowed myself to focus on him and work.

I can read his every movement. I know what he wants before he asks. He said he loves me and that it is my fault that he took me. I ruined my family and his. I am evil, I destroy everything I touch. He drills these things into my head. These comments are harder to push away because I agreed to go with him. It is my fault. I no longer think of running away. It is useless. I will never get away. He is always watching me, and I am always watching him. We develop a silent language that is so subtle nobody else detects it. If we are out and I need to go to the bathroom, we communicate with hand and eye movements. When we are at home if I need to go, it will depend on his mood whether I must ask. If I overstep and do not ask, the consequences are that I am brutally attacked while in the bathroom. It is easier to error on the side of caution and ask. I feel I am slipping away. The sensation of floating and watching myself like a bystander is so comforting. I have heard people speak of when they die. Some can watch what is happening to their body and they feel at peace, feeling only a mild curiosity for the body they left behind. This is happening daily so that I felt numb to any feelings in my body. The brutal attacks could snap me back to reality, but soon I would float up and away again. Perhaps when he hit me with the two by four in the back of my head, maybe my brain was damaged? Whatever it is, I like to slip away from the fear and pain. As I watched on, my physical body becomes more obedient and try ever so hard to please him. My mind chants it's ok, its ok, its ok, its ok, its ok, its ok.

MOM FINDS ME

This is my mother's memory, although I do remember this event. It is like an old black and white movie. I see myself but I have lost the ability to connect with the emotions of who I was? My mother was actively looking for me and moved in the hope of finding me. For so long I was numb to this fact. Only now as I am healing does this fact bring tears to my eyes. I held this memory encased in a tomb, where my heart could not reach. This action said she loved me. I love my mother with all my heart and wanted so much to be loved by her.

I am in Carnegie Mall. I am standing by myself. Kirk and Tara are there but not right beside me. My mother sees me and rushes up to me. She wants me to come with her.

I say "No, I am evil, I am dirty, leave me!"

My mother says no, "I am taking you with me."

I tell her, "Can't you see?! They're watching us!" Kirk comes over, and talks to my mother, though I cannot remember what they say. I think, of course my mom wants to take me. I say no, for I know that he will hurt them, my family.

He says to my mom, "See, she doesn't want to go with you". It is hopeless. I can never leave. Although there is a big gap in my memory, I know Tara and I are no longer close. We are both trying to survive. I forgive Tara so easily because I see her as powerless, like me. We sit in a restaurant, but I can't hear the conversation. I am so terrified for my mother. He has a gun under the table, which he shows her (Handgun). I know later I will be beaten for this episode. It does not occur to me that I might be freed. I have learned to retreat in my mind to the quiet safe place. I must not give into hope, for it will anger him. I remain impassive. I learned long ago that the only way to convince him of my feelings is to convince myself. Seeing my mom makes him crazy. He is always raging like a caged animal. All my privileges will be taken away again. Whatever trust he had built up in me is gone. He needs constant reassurance that I do not want to go back.

He says, "I'm going to kill all of them, your whole fucking family. It is your fault! You will pay for what you have done when I make you watch as I kill all of your family." He slaps me to show me he means it. I have to promise over and over that, if we are caught my name is Rhonda Clairmont and that I will never tell what happened. I try to be convincing, but he never believes me.

MOM

During the kidnapping, my mother moved several times to look for me. I am not sure of how many because we have never talked about it. I must commend her for her determination in looking for me. I now have a daughter and have wondered how I would live with such an experience? I have no idea how? My mother developed her own unique set of coping skills and I know she has endured much worse atrocities than I ever did. She endured a lifetime of kidnapping when I only had to endure a year and a half. Although her anger has been her automatic default emotion, she survived an entire childhood in the residential school. Her anger helped her put one foot in front of the other through many trials in her life. She has shown me how to keep going no matter how bad it gets. I pray one day she will find peace in her heart.

TRAVELLING TO THROW THE POLICE OFF THE TRAIL

My next memory is we are driving in the half ton truck from work. We are in the United States, North Dakota then South Dakota. I am so tired. I am dozing off, smack! He back hands me. I see a flash of light, then I taste blood, my head snaps to attention.

He is screaming and yelling at me. "It's all your fault, don't think you're so f'ing smart!" I do not think I am smart, quite the opposite, really. Would a smart person have put themselves in this position? I am just so tired. He will not let me sleep, and it is taking its toll on both of us. He is getting crazier, and he hits his own head sometimes over and over. Maybe because he is so sleepy too, I'm not sure. Anyhow, he tells me over and over how he has no choice.

He yells "I have to kill you!" I am too tired to care anymore. In the beginning I was scared, but after so long. I can not keep up the kind of terror he wants me to feel.

When I say, "I'm hungry."

He says, "Why would I waste food on you when I'm going to kill you." I really do not know what he wants from me. He is especially angry with my mother whom he calls a dumb cunt. I cannot allow myself to think anything positive, or negative because my facial expressions will give me away. I am beyond trying to avoid his slaps, and punches. He says all the horrible things he is going to do to my sister. In the beginning I was sad, and let tears roll down my eyes. Now I am cried out, and too exhausted. I do not really think about it.

I just quietly tell him, "I'm done, I can not do this anymore." I undo my seat belt. Open the door and let myself fall out of the truck.

Next Memory – we are in a trucker's dinner eating a hamburger and fries. I'm so hungry; I have to slow down because I'm choking from eating so fast. Afterwards, Kirk takes me into a gas station store. He tells me to pick out a postcard. He wants me to write a few words to my mom. I can not remember what I write, but I remember the card has a picture of a rabbit with a monkey tail. I remember thinking it is a magical rabbit. Later in life, I will learn it is a chinchilla.

Kirk was losing his sanity, due to lack of sleep. Tara was so afraid at times that she shook uncontrollably, like a frightened dog. I knew I had reached that state because I was so terrified of what was happening. All his fears had been building over the past two weeks, and as they did, he became more erratic with his thinking and talking to himself. I was also losing my sanity from exhaustion because he would not let me sleep.

GETTING PULLED OVER FOR A TRAFFIC VIOLATION

My next memory is when we returned to Canada. I am in the same truck with Kirk, and Tara. I am in the middle. We are driving under an overpass. A cop car turns on his lights behind us. I am so tired. Kirk curses and pulls over. The police come to his window and ask him for his papers. He gives them over. The policeman tells him his truck is higher than the overpass allows. The cop leaves to go back to his cop car.

He says to Tara, "Get her out of here!" Tara does not know what to do.

He barks at her, "I said get her the fuck out of here!" Tara gets out of the truck. I follow her and get out. We start to walk south away from the truck and the police. We both do not know where to go. We walk up to the lights and cross the street. We see a phone booth and make our way to the phone booth. I am not sure who we were going to call. Both of us are not allowed to have friends or contact with anyone. Suddenly sirens are flashing all around us. We are surrounded by the police.

INTERROGATION

I can not tell the Police, or the Federal Bureau of Investigation, or the Canadian Security Intelligence Service anything. I am so tired. I have not slept in five days. I am so skinny I can feel my ribs, and any loud noises make me jump. Everyone wants to talk to me, or stare at me like I am a freak or something. I feel very alone and anxious in the police station. The police are trying to get me to admit that I am Sky Sparrowhawk. They know who I am. I will not tell and put my sister in danger, I am Rhonda Clairmont. They keep switching interrogators. I think they hope one of them will get through to me. I can feel him all around me. They can't protect me. No one can. Now they try to send in a female officer. She tells me she is from the FBI. She may as well be a guy because she loses her patience and slams her fist on the table before walking out. I try to take a nap, but they will not let me. They slam books on the table to make loud enough noises to wake me up. I break because I am so tired, and I can not take it anymore. I feel like the interrogation is going into somewhere between five and eight hours. My exhaustion is distorting time.

I tell them, "If you can keep my sister safe, I will tell you what happened." He threatened to do so many horrible things to her. I can not live with myself if he hurt her, because of me. She is younger and I know he would take her if he can get to her.

They take my sister and fly her to Nova Scotia to my dad. In a few hours they have her on the phone and let me talk to her.

I ask her, "Where are you?" She says, "I am at Dads." I am so relieved.

She asks me, "Are you okay?"

I say, "Yes, I'm okay. I have to talk to the police now."

After we hang up. I am relieved and I answer their questions finally. After a while they can see I keep falling asleep. They bring me to my mom's apartment. There is a mattress on the living room floor. I hug my mom; we sit at the table and try to talk. She can see I'm tired, and she lets me sleep. I have been awake five days without sleep, I am barely coherent anymore. When I awake my Mom says I was sleeping for 14 hours straight. Finally, I feel I can function and talk again. They let me know they let him go. Because they could only hold him for so many hours. They said there will be a court date later, but he is no longer in custody. They will gather evidence. Good, I hope and pray he will just go away!

I am assigned bodyguards until the court date. One day I am in a store with my mom, and I came out. I am waiting for my mom since she is still in the store. The two bodyguards are standing close by talking. I see Kirk, he is watching me, but he knows that the bodyguards are there. He motions with his head for me to come. My heart is pounding, and I shiver. I am so scared. I can't breathe for a minute. I stand there frozen. When he realizes I am not going to come to him, he vanishes.

Although I did not go with him, I feel that we have a bond. It is painful for me to let him go. Later, I will learn about Stockholm Syndrome. I do not want him to suffer for taking me. I thought he was trying to protect me. I made many excuses for him and the level of violence he inflicted upon me, because he said he loved me. It would take many years for me to learn to appreciate love given without violence. I had come to rely on being told what to do and it was hard for me to feel safe doing anything without anyone telling me it was ok first. Going to the washroom was the hardest. I had become accustomed to asking even if I did not say it out loud, since we communicated with hand signals, and body language. Nobody could understand when I asked to go to the washroom. They would tell me in frustration, "You don't have to ask!" They could not understand that it was necessary for me at the time. I had been programmed to obey. Freedom is a state of mind. My body has been freed but my mind remained imprisoned.

MEDICAL EXAMINATION

I am told I need to go to the hospital for a pelvic exam. They want to have proof of intercourse. I am brought to the University Hospital. I am in a room and asked to undress and get on the table.

A nurse asks me, "Is it ok to let the doctor come inside? I shyly nod. The doctor comes in.

He asks me, "Is it ok for some students to be in the room? I cannot say no because I have never been allowed to say no in my life. I am twelve years old.

"Yes," I whisper, because I am terrified, and my bottom is bare. I can barely breathe. I use this trick when things get too hard. I take slow careful breaths through my mouth. The doctor and six students are looking at my privates, and the doctor is telling them kidnapping stuff explaining stuff about my sexual parts, but I cannot hear. It is taking everything for me to just breathe. Creator! I don't want to be here. I start to rise out of my body and float away. The doctor's voice gets muffled and quiet. I come back later when it is finished. I have a huge mistrust of doctors for most of my life. Only in the last two years have I finally gotten over my fear of them. I see a lot of people go to doctors a lot sooner than I would. I must be forced before I can get up the nerve to see a doctor.

SENT HOME TO LIVE WITH MOM/NOT WORKING OUT

Mom and I do not get along. I am angry at her all the time. She drinks and has another creepy boyfriend who leers at me. I start to drink with her, and we erupt into fights. Then she kicks me out and calls the cops and says I ran away. I rekindle my friendship with Lexi, my older cousin. Sometimes I go to her place. Sometimes I look for an unlocked car to crawl into, or a stairwell to stay warm. After a couple of months, I am put into foster care.

FOSTER CARE

In foster care, I am the youngest teen. There are two older boys seventeen, and eighteen, and an older girl who is seventeen also. They seem noticeably confident. I feel awkward and dirty beside them. The house is beautiful. My room is full of beautiful white furniture. The living room has a white carpet and expensive furniture. We are only allowed in there to receive adult guests.

The psychiatrist I see has prescribed Zoloft, an antidepressant. I am forced to take it. The drug makes me hallucinate and I see monsters come out of people's faces. Sometimes it is Kirk's face morphing out of the faces of others. When I hallucinate, I strike out and fight out of fear. I do not know what's happening to me. I can't control myself. I have been dropped into a perfect world that I am screwing up. I used to think the Brady Bunch was not real. Now I know it is, but I don't fit in that world. I am broken. The other teens don't like me. They whisper mean things when they think no one can hear. Why are you faking? You are so annoying. We cannot stand you. I hope you get taken away. I have learned to stay silent; it is the safest thing to do. I think the oldest boy is the kindest to me. He is eighteen and he is quiet. One day when everyone is gone, he pokes his head out of the closet. He motions for me to come and see something in the closet. I go over and walk in with him. He pulls me to him and starts kissing me. He pulls open my shirt and is touching me, He drops his pants and whacks off. I pull away and get out of the closet. I run to my room and put a chair in front of it. I say nothing. He will no longer talk to me or acknowledge me. I am dirty.

COURT

I am forced to see a psychiatrist, and a psychologist. The psychologist brings me to court. She tells me that the court room will be cleared for my case because I am a minor. There will only be the Judge, Kirk, the stenographer, and a security guard.

The psychologist asks me if I want her to go into the court room with me.

I shyly say, "I want to go in alone," hoping she will not be offended. I am ashamed for anyone to know what happened.

She says, "That's fine." I am called to go in. I walk into the courtroom. Once in the court room I see a teacher, with a class of kids. I believe they are older than me. I am in shock, seeing all the kids, is making me lightheaded and I drift away. Not sure where, but far away from the prying eyes burning into my filthy flesh. I believe I may be having a mental breakdown. I run to the corner and put my head into the corner and cry, I am completely overwhelmed. I want to scream, but I can't. The courtroom is cleared. I am brought to the front. Kirk is not there. Later, they tell me they issued a warrant for his arrest. If he is ever caught, I will be called in again.

I ask, "What if it's 20 years from now?" They say they would still contact me and let me review my statement in case I forget anything. I am 12 years old.

SCHOOL

My foster parents are registering me for school. They buy me new clothes and bedding. At the school I cannot seem to focus, think, or talk. I am distracted and anxious. I stare out the window most of the time. I do not make any friends. I feel like everyone knows and is whispering about me. The teacher gives up on me and I am told I will be going to another school. The next school is for mentally challenged kids. I know there is something wrong with me, but I also know I do not belong at this school. My thoughts are jumbled, and I cannot stay with a thought. I am confused and overwhelmed, but I am not mentally challenged. I feel like I am locked away in my mind and can't find my way out because I don't know what I need, or even if I did, how to say it. Silence has always kept me safe. Old patterns are hard to break.

CHOOSING TO LIVE ON THE STREETS: HOMELESS

started to drink and do drugs. I did not like the drugs the psychiatrist gave me Zoloft (now proven to be dangerous). The pills made me hallucinate and see demons come out of people's faces. My cousin Lexi believed that smoking weed and drinking alcohol was better. I ran away and stayed with Lexi for a while and it was great in the beginning. Later we fought, and she shacked up with a boyfriend. Slowly I spent more and more time on the streets. At first, I slept on people's couches and then eventually in stairwells, under bridges, unlocked vehicles, and behind dumpsters. Once I snuck into a retirement home and slept behind a sofa in their common area. I scared those old people when I just stood up and walked out the next morning. One night a man and his wife offered to take me in. I went to their place only to find they wanted me to take my clothes off to sleep on their couch. I obeyed even though a little voice said do not do it. After a while I awoke to them asking me to crawl into bed with them. I grabbed my clothes and ran, leaving behind my sneakers. I learned to lie constantly to survive because I was underage and would be locked up if I did not. I was thirteen years old.

WILL

I met a man much older when I was fourteen and he was twenty-eight. His name was Will. He was in and out of prison. I was in juvenile detention twice and prison once. We would be on again off again for seven years. Back then, we were drawn together like moths to a flame. He was attractive in a Cory Heart/Rod Stewart kind of way. When I first met him, I disliked his arrogance and boastfulness. He disliked my style of clothing and believed I should use the assets I had been blessed with. I preferred solid colours rather than the flashy bold clothes he wore. Later when we became involved, he picked out my clothes and oversaw my hairstyles.

After one of my trips to the stylist, he freaked out and screamed and yelled at the stylist. Refusing to pay, he said that she had ruined my hair, and cut too much off. I was so humiliated but said nothing. He said he was accustomed to dating fashionable women. The eighties were outrageous, and I struggled at first to wear the mini skirts, and leather outfits he preferred to see me in, not to mention the high heels.

Time after time we found each other when we got out of jail and detention lock up. You would think I'd had enough violence in my past that I would try to avoid violent people. I believed he loved me and if I just loved him enough, he would learn to be peaceful and loving. Will's mother had abandoned him as a child, and then he went into foster care. The first time he hit me I left for days, but I had nowhere to go. He apologized and I went back to him. Over time he became more possessive and controlling. As I became older, I learned to fight back.

FIGHTING BACK

One night in a hotel room he backhanded me, and I fell to the floor. I tasted blood. He walked into the bathroom and when he came out, I was standing. He was naked. I was half dressed because I was heading out to get us some take out food. He was about to punch me. I could see his fist ball up as he was screaming in my face. Something about listening to him, if only I would listen, he would not have to hit me. I do not know what possessed me to do it, but I grabbed a hold of his privates and squeezed. I had long nails at the time, and it must have hurt because he didn't hit me. When he started to yell and call me down, I gave a squeeze and a little twist. It felt so good to be able to fight back for once.

Then he said, "You better enjoy this moment because, when I get my hands on you, You're fuckin dead!" I was stuck, how was I going to get away! I knew as soon as I let go, he would jump me.

He said, "You better run far, because I'll be coming for you!" The hotel room was his. I was too young to get a room by myself. So, I would have to go. I already had my pants on. I slipped a t-shirt over my head but never let go. My shirt was not completely on but would have to do until I got away. I slipped my shoes on pulling him by his penis so that he would not hit me. He threatened me every step of the way.

At one point he pleaded, "Come on baby just let go, you know I love you. I'm not going to hurt you, just let go." I had been hit enough in my life to know it was bullshit. I collected my purse and jacket. I decided socks were not necessary! I eased him over to the door and told him that I just wanted to get out of there. He wanted me to just let him go. He started cursing and threatening again. I opened the door to get ready to run, but I just knew he would grab me and beat the living shit out of me. I did the only thing I could think of. I gave his privates the biggest squeeze and twist that I could. I saw him double over, and his eyes roll back a bit, Then I knew, I had a small window to run! I ran like the wind, or so I thought. I am sure I was clumsier than I thought for I was high and drunk at the time.

LOCKED UP

The first time I was locked up was for obstruction of justice which meant I lied about my name so that they would not take me back to the foster home. Eventually I was taken back to the foster home and the same boy James was there. I ran away a few days later. James glared daggers at me every time he looked at me. The foster family was in the process of adopting him. He told me silently with his eyes that he would destroy me if I messed that up for him.

One night I was alone, and it was cold outside. Will was in Jail. I lined up at the homeless shelter and signed in for a bed. As I curled up to go to sleep my hand slipped under the pillow, there I found a bag of pills. I took them with me in the morning when I left. I decided to go and look them up at the library. I read up on them and decided they were safe. I downed a couple of the pills and when they didn't seem to have an effect, I downed a couple more. I blacked out and came to in the security office of the Hudson Bay. I had been shoplifting and the security guard was taking clothing items out of my bag. I tried to convince him each item he took out was mine. Then he would show me the price tag. One sweater did not have a tag, and he put it back into my bag.

My mother showed up in court and said she did not know what to do with me. I believe I was fourteen when I was sent to a detention lock up. Back then, children had no rights. I was told this by an orderly when I tried to demand a phone call. I was also told they could hold me for however long they wanted if I was considered a (danger to myself, or society). This meant I had to be evaluated by the psychiatrist every couple of weeks. He prescribed antidepressants and sleeping pills. I didn't mind the sleeping pill. I've always had a hard time sleeping. Although I was in constant pursuit of pain relief, to erase the memories, I did not like someone else dictating to me when and how many drugs to take. The drugs they gave me, made me feel like a walking zombie. During my time in detention my aunt Mary visited me once while she was passing through. I appreciated it immensely. I was stubborn and vowed I would not stay in there until I was 18. I had heard from others that if I got out and was able to stay out of trouble, get a place and support myself, they would leave me alone. I could go to the child welfare and tell them I had a job and was taking care of myself. I vowed to break out of detention and learn to take care of myself. I made two attempts to break out.

BREAK OUT

My first attempt was during an evening outing to a swimming pool right next door. The walk to and from the pool was a short distance outside beyond the gated fence of the detention centre where we were held. Another girl named Eva was going to make a run for it also. When the time came, we bolted. Both of us ran first together for a short distance, then when we saw a guard chasing us, we separated. Later we found each other and hid in a garage till the cold became unbearable. A few hours had passed, and we figured we might be in the clear. Unfortunately, the lady guard that chased us had broken her leg and the other guards were determined to find us. We had made it to a main road, and it was around one o clock in the morning when we stuck out our thumbs. A few cars passed. When the fourth car slowed down, we were excited until we saw the doors open. Both of us bolted again in different directions but were tackled by huge men. Later I learned that one of the men was the husband of the lady guard that broke her leg. I was sorry for the woman who broke her leg as a result of our breakout attempt.

I was then sent to a higher security lock up. This lock up was situated in the middle of a huge field that would take you a hard run of a half hour to reach the perimeter. If anyone tried to make a run for it, the guards would only have to hop in a car and drive around to pick you up. They also had a tier system in place so that only the highest tier could walk outside of the fence. It would take months to get to the highest tier, since you had to be obedient to all staff. Refraining from any serious disputes with the other inmates was a little more challenging. There were cliques and I struggled to stay out of the cliques which meant I was a lone wolf. After a few months of good behavior, I was able to get a job in the kitchen and was able to start generating an income. I could take a special snack for myself after cleaning up. Eventually, I would take a couple extra snacks and sell them to the girls for cash. Cash was hard to come by because they had a canteen. The canteen was run on a credit system. But I knew eventually when I got out, I would need cash. I never knew what my plans were, but I knew I had to be a model prisoner and try to accumulate as much cash as I could. As I worked my way up the tier levels, I started to feel safe and secure. I should have stayed there, but I was a stubborn willful child, I entered a new phase of life in which I hated being told when to eat, sleep, shower.

Eventually the time came when I had reached the highest tier level. I had been in detention for nine months. At the highest tier level, you could walk outside the gates unaccompanied because they thought that the field was so big. They had cameras and would be able to see, and apprehend you, should you make a run for it. The other privilege that I had been given was to make a phone call unsupervised to my mom. The phone was in an office with a glass partition. In the adjoining room the guard was handing out afternoon meds. I had already signed up for an unaccompanied walk.

I asked the guard, "Could I quickly call my mom before I went on my walk?"

She said, "Yes, go ahead." Normally she would dial it, but because she was busy, she nodded to me. I slipped the number out and sat down to make the call. I hoped she would not hear me. I was so scared and nervous.

The phone rang and the lady on the other end said, "Yellow

Taxi, what is your address please?" I gave the address as quickly and quietly as I dared.

The dispatch lady said, "Right away ma'am, 15-20 minutes".

I hung up the phone and waved to the guard, letting her know I was going out for my walk. I was shaky and scared. I had not let any of the other girls know my intentions because I didn't want to get anyone else in trouble. The last attempt had gotten Eva into trouble and I felt horrible about it. This time I had to go alone. I felt slightly guilty because I had grown to like the staff. I just could not bear the thought of being locked up a few more years. I wanted to be free. Once outside I was fidgety, tying and untying my shoelace. In the front of the building there was a circular driveway with a parking lot off to the side where the staff parked. I walked very slowly watching for the taxi and trying to look calm for the security cameras in case I was being watched. When the Yellow Taxi came into view, I had to slow my breathing down. It took all my restraint to wait until it was a little closer to the circular driveway, before walking towards the taxi. If the cameras were watching, I didn't want to alert anyone of my intentions until that last minute. I also didn't know whether the taxi driver would know this was a detention lock up and whether or not he would refuse to take me. I had to look calm. As he pulled up in front of the building, I arrived at the front. I hopped in and he asked me where I was going. I was not sure, so I said downtown, please. I knew we were on the outskirts of the city and I was not sure how much money it would take. I let him know there was a big tip If he hurried, because I was in a rush. He said ok and took off. I watched as we left, so far no one was running out. I continued to look out the back as we drove away. Different scenarios started to run through my head. What if they called him on the radio and told him to bring me back, or to the police station. Finally, we were going past one of the suburbs of the city. I saw a train station and told the taxi to pull into the city train station. I had sixty- two dollars. The taxi was twelve dollars and change, I told him it would be faster for me to take the train. I gave him a twenty for a tip. I knew he would get in trouble, or at least have a lot of questions to answer. I said thank you and ran for the next train. Once on the train, I still did not think I was in the clear. I made it to the centre of downtown and exited the train, losing myself in the crowd and watching over my shoulder every few minutes. After a few blocks I started to relax. Nobody was following me. I had done it and I was free. All I had to do was stay out of trouble and try to be smarter. I set out to find Will. If I were smarter, I would have stayed away from Will, but they say people find their level of insanity just like water finds its level when two fluids join. He accepted me for who I was, and I accepted him, violence, flaws, and all. Who was I to judge him, I was just as messed up as him? Plus, I was underage and although I could put on a good front, I did not really know how to survive on my own.

Over the years, Will and I ended up using harder and harder drugs. He was battling his demons as was I. We lived on skid row for many years. I preferred to become an invisible person. I hated myself and was in such a dark place that I did not even believe I had the right to pray. I imagined that God hated me. Will was the opposite of me, he was flashy and needed to be seen and heard. He was attractive in a swaggering kind of way.

One drunken night as we argued, I crossed the street to get away from him, and I was hit by a car. I awoke in the hospital to a man crying at my bedside. I assumed he was the one who hit me. I told him not to worry I was sore but felt I would be ok. The doctor said I needed to use crutches for six weeks afterwards. Will was not around the hospital when I came to. He said he called the police, and my mother. Then he took off because he had a warrant out for his arrest. My mother came and checked me out of the hospital. To her credit, she did not send me back to lock-up. I stayed with her while I was recuperating. She lived in an apartment basement unit. One night we heard a knock on the living room window. I opened the curtain to see Will drenched because it was raining. My mother had already instructed me that I was not to let him in, should he show up. Will became angry and demanded to be let in, shaking his fist at me. Again, I said no! By this time, my mother had heard the noise and had come into the living room. Then, Will punched the window and glass shattered everywhere. He was screaming and yelling at me, and he tried to grab me. He was too late. I had backed up to avoid the shattering glass. My mother screamed and yelled at him to get out. She attacked like a Pitbull, jumping with superhuman strength up and through the window. She chased Will and grabbed the back of his jacket just as he was running through a big puddle. Down he went with a splash! She kicked and clawed at him as he tried to get up and run. I could not believe my eyes. She had him on the run. I could not help but be proud of her. When she came back, she was breathing heavily, I tried to conceal my smile. Back then, she did not hug or say I love you, but her attack on Will said she cared. Eventually Will and I got back together. I was in love with him and his cruel ways, perhaps because I had only experienced painful love. Even though I loathed his arrogance and his need to take control of any room he went into. It was intriguing to me. I guess a part of me was attracted to what I thought was confidence at the time. Perhaps some of it could rub off on me?

A NEW START

At age fifteen when Will and I got back together, he wanted to make a fresh start. This meant moving to another province. When he had a plan stuck in his head, he was relentless. I agreed and told him I knew how to hop trains. We gathered provisions, sleeping bags, tarp, and a water canteen as well as sandwiches and a transistor radio. Off we went to the next province over, Saskatchewan. Halfway there, the train slowed. We got off to replenish our water supply and decided to camp overnight. We laid the tarp down then the sleeping bag and covered the rest of the tarp over us. I felt safe and loved.

Upon arriving in the city, we headed downtown, and he spoke about getting a lay of the land. I did not know exactly what that meant but probably money and drugs I figured. He told me to wait in a park and come back to a certain street corner at 4:00 pm. I was nervous because I felt an unnatural attachment to him. Perhaps it was the residual effects of the kidnapping. I felt anxiety when I had to leave him. The only time I did not get that feeling was when I was mad at him. When I returned to the corner, he had shown me, he was nowhere in sight. I was a little nervous but waited. An hour passed and it started to rain. Luckily, he had bought me a rain poncho. Forty-five minutes later I could hear my name being called, but I couldn't see him anywhere. Strange? I walked a little way to try to see if I was hearing correctly. I heard it again SKyyyyyy! I cocked my strongest hearing ear up and took off the hood of my poncho. I closed my eyes to try and pinpoint where it was coming from. The voice signalled me to look up. I scanned the buildings around me. Then I saw it, an arm waving out a window? What the hell?

He yelled out that he was in jail. I felt like I was punched in the stomach, it hurt so bad. He had told me several days before that if he went to jail it would be a minimum of 1 year.

Great, I was alone in a city I did not know. I could not go home. My mom was already sick and tired of me going back to him when she knew he was violent. Also, I foolishly listened to him and let him take, and cash one of my moms checks from her check book. I knew it was wrong, but not the impact it could have on my mom. She was forced to lay charges, or else she would be in trouble. In any case she was livid. I had only talked to her on the phone and knew she was fed up with me and Will. I brought it on myself. I was slowly painting myself into a corner, with fewer and fewer options. I cried for a couple of hours, feeling sorry for myself. Then I found myself in a park on a bench, wondering what to do. I was 15 about to turn 16, sober and straight, with no drugs on me. I only had a few dollars to my name. I knew I had some relatives here in Saskatoon but how would I find them? I decided my best bet would be to try to find phone numbers.

DENISE

I went to a phone booth and dialed 411 for information. A lady with a kind voice answered. I asked for the names of the few relatives I knew that lived there. There was nothing listed, and I didn't know what to do. The lady on the other end was very patient and seemed to know I was upset. She took the time to talk to me and ask what the matter was. I spilled out my predicament. I had come here with a guy and he had been arrested and now I was in a big city and had no place to go. She listened and offered to help. I could not believe it. She said when she got off work, she would come and help me. I was so relieved. She asked me where I was, and I told her. She described the directions to a MacDonald's that was a couple of miles away. I told her that I could find it and described what I was wearing, so she would recognize me. Then we arranged to meet there in a few hours. It was a decent walk to get there, but I was feeling optimistic. It did not seem far considering at the end, I would be in the company of someone kind and caring. Before we hung up, she introduced herself as Denise and said that she would see me when she got off work.

I had butterflies in my stomach when I got there and waited. She introduced herself again, and although I felt shy, I tried to be open and friendly. Usually, I let Will do the talking, so it was a challenge to force myself to act grownup and confident. I did not tell her my real age for fear she would hand me over to the authorities. I told her I was 18. I'm not sure if she believed me, probably not. After talking for awhile, she offered to let me come to her place and sleep on her sofa. I was a little apprehensive since I'd had a previous experience when a couple had offered me a place to stay and wanted sex. I had no choice. It was raining, and I did not have the tarp and sleeping bag. I could try to find a shelter, but this new city had me freaked out. It smelled different and seemed ominous without Will. I would give this a chance. She was there in a little blue Toyota. She reminded me of Delta Burke, the actress, I instantly liked her. She asked me questions as we drove into the twilight. I tried to answer as honestly as I could, without giving away any incriminating facts like my real age. Never had I seen such selflessness in a human. Denise wanted to take care of me. She knew I was timid, and she respected my awkwardness. She only had a 1-bedroom apartment, so she made up the couch for me to sleep on. The next morning, she made breakfast and I helped in any way that I could with her cleaning chores, and laundry. She prayed before she ate her food and at night before we went to sleep. She got down on her knees and prayed for me. It made me nervous to pray with her, for I thought that I had done something bad for God to have allowed my life to be so painful. I believed everything was my fault, and I was evil.

The next day was Sunday and it was kind of a blur. We went to church and when the pastor asked if anyone needed prayers, Denise rose and shared what little I had told her and asked for donations of clothes for me. Although I was so moved by her generosity, I was also afraid of being in the spotlight. I felt like fainting in the church. Everything seemed so big and I felt like everyone was staring at me. I tried not to let the tears well up, but I couldn't help it. I excused myself and went to the bathroom and hid. I did not come out for a while until I could compose myself. I was ashamed of my tears. She had said goodbye to most of her friends by then and we could go. She had no idea of the trauma I had endured and was acting out of the goodness of her heart. I didn't know how to explain my tears and said nothing.

She said they had prayed and would be praying for me. I had no words, only silent tears that slipped down my face once again. I felt so unworthy. Throughout the weekend people dropped by to donate clothing for me. I had a hard time looking people in the eye when I thanked them. On Monday she went back to work all day and I completed all the chores she asked of me. By Tuesday I had decided to leave. I cleaned the apartment as best as I could and took a plastic bag with a couple of changes of clothes. I left Denise a note thanking her and letting her know that it was nothing she did, she was the kindest person I have ever met. I didn't know how to explain anything else, so I didn't. Now looking back, I can see that I felt so unworthy that I did not deserve the love and kindness she gave. Also, the drug and alcohol cravings that gave relief from the memories were creeping back into my mind.

I went downtown and found a group of homeless people drinking from a bottle, which was some Lysol and water concoction. They recognized me as one of their own and offered me a drink. I took a drink, and it burned my throat. Though the taste was horrible, I knew it would take me away from the pain of looking at myself. I went back to sleeping in cars and stairwells and consuming whatever drugs I could get my hands on. Eventually, I got a hold of a tarp and sleeping bag which I wrapped up and hid in a park under some bushes. I walked far from downtown so that my stash (tarp and sleeping bag) would not be found and stolen from me. There were places to get showers and soup lines for food, so I learned to migrate with the crowd to the best places for free food and clothing. At one of the drop-in places there was a message board to post notes up for other homeless people.

I checked the board daily after my shower to see if Will was out looking for me. One day one of the workers asked me where I was originally from, I told him Lox Reservation. He said that he was from there as well and that his name was Simon. We got to talking and it turned out he was my cousin. Small world! One day when I came into the drop in, he said his wife Rae, was looking for a babysitter. Her brother, who was their babysitter had gotten another job. I said sure I could. He brought me back to his place to meet her. I liked her immediately. She was a straight hip shooter. Rae always got to the point quickly and was very direct. She was a lady who knew what she wanted and didn't mince words. She explained all the duties in a matter of fact way. Then she spoke about my sleeping arrangements.

"You may sleep on the couch for now until I clean out this large closet, then we can put a small bed in here for you." A twin-size bed fit in the closet. I liked her no-nonsense approach. I felt at ease in her company. She never asked questions that made me squirm or feel sad. I played with their children and cleaned the house during the day. I don't know why but I did not crave drugs or alcohol, I felt happy and loved the kids. They were a joy to be around and I let my defenses down. I never cooked because Rae was such a good cook. I knew my food would not be appetizing to this family who was used to her gourmet meals. I did the dishes after the meal and enjoyed watching the family banter in front of the television in the evening before bed.

One day Simon brought a message back from the drop-in Centre. Will was out! He was looking for me. Although I was happy where I was, I missed Will. I loved him and was so excited. I left the cozy life I had created to go back to the streets to look for Will. I enjoyed being with Simon and Rae's family, but I wanted my own. I thought Will and I would be together forever, and someday starting our own family. Will was waiting at the park where he said he would be, and when I saw him, I ran and jumped into his arms. He swung me around, hugging me, shouting, and tearing up. I did too. I had missed him so much it physically hurt. All my anger towards him for leaving me, dissipated. Joy and tears gave way to laughter and poking. He had a rooming house, so we went there and were blissful for a couple of days before he ran out of drugs and reality came crashing back. His love for me gave way to his need for drugs and soon he was plotting his next big score.

During this time, we both progressed to injecting needles in our arms. Eventually he would end up in jail again, and I would be left with the rooming house. This time I was a little wiser. I had learned to sell the different prescription pills and Ts and Rs which is slang for, "Talwin and Ritalin a combination that is injected and produces an effect similar to the effect of heroin mixed with cocaine" (Jones, *Drug slang dictionary - words starting with t* 2021). I was not mature enough or disciplined enough to be a good dealer. I barely scraped by because I was more interested in feeding my own addiction.

The front desk manager of the rooming house took a shine to me and let me work the front for some of my rent. I could tell it was only a matter of time before he tried to sleep with me. It creeped me out the way he looked at me and I knew he had the master keys to all the rooms. At night I put a chair under my door as extra insurance. One night he let himself into my room and I was forced to scream and yell at him. I knew I needed to scare him. I was able to become the bear I needed to, and it worked. He staggered out of my room and never tried to enter again without permission. The next day we both acted like it had never happened. I should have left but I was barely scraping by and I needed any extra to go to my drug use.

Looking back, I can now see that my ability to feel fear was distorted. I did not assess danger in a way that could keep me safe. I had witnessed and lived through so much violence that it desensitized me. The years of floating away (disassociation) to protect myself from the pain coupled with drugs and alcohol left me emotionally numb. I had barely escaped with my life and witnessed many sisters who were not so lucky. It was a slow transition to leave the streets and drugs that helped me to escape the pain of my past. Learning to love myself felt like some airy-fairy words made up for privileged children who came from loving and safe homes. They say you must hit rock bottom, and it's different for everyone. For me rock bottom came in stages.

Stage one was coming to the realization that I wanted to live. I discovered I wanted to live upon waking up in a hotel with a needle hanging out of my arm. I had been used sexually for a few days by a group of men that were drug dealers and possibly, their friends. I tried to stand but could not. I fell to the floor. I realized then that if I didn't get out of that room, I would probably die there. I had hazy memories of trying to leave and the men injecting me with more drugs. I crawled to the door on my elbows, and used all my strength to open the door, and call for help. Someone saw me and called an ambulance. I would love to say that was my last time using and my life magically turned around. It was not. For many, it takes a few times through the recovery door before an addiction is left behind. I never told anyone of the experience of waking up in the hotel that way. It has been hard to make peace with this and forgive myself. Stage two for me was asking for help. It was one of the hardest things for me to do, even to this day. I must admit that I don't remember very much of my hard drug use because has been over 30 years since I injected a needle in my arm. I do remember the taste that hit the back of my throat and the feeling of peace that came over me seconds later. During that time period, I was constantly craving the peace that lifted me out of the shame and self hatred I felt.

AARON

Aaron was much older and in his fifties. He was a building contractor, and a workaholic who lived alone. Will was in jail once again. I was living in a different rooming house downtown with a shared bathroom and kitchen. I met Aaron in a park across the street from a building he was working on. He sat down at the same bench where I was, to eat his bagged lunch. He struck up a conversation and we became friends. It seemed he was a loner, and wanted to connect with someone, just as I did. It was not long before we became lovers. Will had been in and out of jail during our relationship and I felt like we were drifting apart. I resented him always leaving me. I did not feel like I could count on him anymore. Aaron drank alcohol but never used any type of drugs and didn't want to be around them. I was careful not to use them around him. I tried on my own to kick them but I was always scared of the withdrawals.

Aaron said, "If you really want to, you can do it." When I visited him, he encouraged me and told me his door was always open. My visits to his place became longer as time went by. He told me he loved me and wanted me to stay but not the drugs.

He had a fully stocked bar and said, "I don't mind you drinking to your heart's content, but no drugs."

I warned him of the consequences, "I will not be a pretty sight once I go into withdrawals." He assured me he could handle it. I confided in Aaron about a few stories from my past and he would hold me when I cried. I knew Will would be getting out of jail soon and I had to be honest with Aaron.

I told Aaron, "I care deeply for you, but I do not know if I am able to be in a relationship the way you want." I confessed that I felt this pull to be with Will even though he treated me badly and I did not know if it was love. If it was, it was a painful kind of love that was euphoric at times. When we clashed the hurt and heartbreak was excruciating.

I really don't know what precipitated the end of my drug use. Perhaps it was the unconditional love and kindness Aaron showed me. He cooked, and cleaned, and helped me in every way through it. All my cursing and vomiting and crying is what I remember most. The physical withdrawals were so painful, my arms felt like they were beaten with a baseball bat. He took time off work and nursed me through my withdrawal symptoms. I still cannot believe he was able to stand me because I treated him so badly through it. He had a fully stocked bar and kept it stocked for me daily. He told me months later that Will had came looking for me. He chased him off after a violent confrontation. He kept it from me because he knew that Will would have offered me drugs to ease my pain and I would have left with him.

He was right, I would have I'm ashamed to say. It was my choice to get clean and stay clean, but any temptations during that time could have easily derailed me, as they had in the past attempts. Once I finally got clean, I had to stay away from the skids for a while. Aaron knew this, I am not sure how probably from my previous attempts. I was worried about the room I rented. He went and gathered my things and paid the rent. I did not want to let the place go in case we got into a fight, though he seemed to love me, and would not fight no matter how irritated or grouchy I became. Although he did not live in a flashy place, he didn't seem to worry about money. I tried to stay cheery because it seemed that was all he really wanted from me. He also wanted me to stay away from drugs. I wanted that too, and I was smart enough to know how my body would start to react when it was around. They called me, taunting me with the old familiar sensations. One day Will showed up when Aaron was gone. I agreed to take a walk with him. He looked terrible and needed money. I gave him what I had. I thought he was coming to get me. When he asked me to go with him, I hesitated only slightly. It was strange because he called me an idiot. I would have expected him to get mad because of my hesitation.

He said, "You have a great set up, this guy is in love with you! You have him eating out of your palm."

I cried "I thought you loved me."

He said, "I will come back for you when I am set up with a place and a bag." In the meantime, I was to get as much money from Aaron as I could get. I was suddenly furious at Will for abandoning me. How many times he had left me to fend for myself and now this. He did not know how I suffered while he was away. Now, he wanted me to hurt the one person who had been so kind to me.

I screamed, "I will not!" I stomped away! He came running after me and grabbed me by the hair, kissing me long and hard.

When he released me, he said, "Yes you will do as you're told because I love you, and you love me. Say it!" I repeated what he said with tears in my eyes. I felt the knots in my stomach and the drug cravings coming back. At the time, the drugs were the only thing in the world that offered me peace from my painful past, and all the voices that told me I was bad, I was unlovable, I was weak, and I would never amount to anything. I deserved everything I had lived through, and more.

Later that night when Aaron returned home, I confessed to him everything that Will had instructed me to do. Aaron knew I was weak, and still he cared and wanted to help me. He suggested we fly home to visit my mother. I was so excited! He booked us first class tickets and we stayed in a fancy hotel. Once there, he met my mother and stepfather. They could see that he had money and was kind to me. My mother was happy I was with someone who did not hurt me, even though he was so much older. Growing up she stressed the importance of finding a man with a good job. Will never worked an honest day in his life, so she called him down every chance she got. When we returned, Will had disappeared, and I didn't see him for quite some time.

BRIAN'S GIFT

O ne night I had a dream that I was meeting my brother Brian in a park. He told me they are coming! He was frantic and in a hurry. I asked him if I could come with him to meet them.

He said, "No, just go! You can't be here when they get here!" I was concerned and tried to keep talking to him, but he stuffed some paper in my hands and pushed me.

He yelled my name, Sky. I suddenly woke up and I jumped out of bed and ran around to the windows to see if he was there. It seemed so real. I was confused. Tears came to my eyes and slipped out, and I was filled with a deep sense of sadness. The next day when I checked the message board, I saw urgent messages from my aunt Mary to call her. When I called, she explained that she and my other aunt Etta were searching the skid row bars for me. There was a family emergency and she wanted to pick me up to bring me home.

I said, "Just tell me."

"It's not something I can say on the phone," She replied.

I could not hold back any longer.

I blurted out, "Brian's dead." She paused for a moment and asked me if someone had told me, but I said no one had." She arranged to pick me up and bring me back for the funeral. Brian's death was ruled a suicide by shot gun.

As soon as I got back home, I saw my grandmother Ellie. I told her of my dream about Brian. She asked what the sun was doing in my dream. I told her the sun was setting it was twilight but turning dark fast. She also asked what he put in my hand and I told her it was paper; I had not looked at it. So, I was not sure.

She said, "Your brother came to give you a parting gift, it will come in the form of paper. You must remember to say some prayers and thank him when you get this gift." I assured her that I would and then put it out of my mind for the moment. Brian was buried in the exact spot we had run away to as children, the very spot we had said we wished we could stay forever. His death was especially hard on my mom, but I was in too much pain to be supportive to her.

I returned to the city quickly after his death and went back to Aaron and his fully stocked bar. I leaned heavily on alcohol to relieve my guilt. I had stopped in to see Brian a few months earlier and he had asked if he could stay with me for a bit. I had said no because I could not even take care of myself. I was still a mess then and I didn't want him to see me like that. Perhaps if I said yes, he might be alive. I am sure we all blame ourselves when a suicide in our family occurs.

Aaron was very loving, attentive, patient and kind. After he got home from work he would cook and clean and cuddle with me as I wept and felt sorry for myself. It was customary for him to fill out lottery ticket forms for the 649 draws. As a courtesy he had me fill out forms too. One day he came in all excited and said that I'd won five hundred dollars. I was not that thrilled because I thought he had won and was trying to give me his win to cheer me up. When he showed me the form, I was confused. I had never won anything before. Brian was the lucky one! He nicknamed me Charlie Brown because I was so unlucky! Then I remembered the dream and what my grandmother had said about the dream. It was his parting gift. I did as my grandmother said, prayed and thanked my brother for protecting me and being there for me. Somehow knowing he was able to give me a parting gift helped to ease my guilt. For if he blamed me, he would not have gifted me.

Although Aaron was so much older, I felt like I loved him in a much different way than I loved Will. Aaron asked me to marry him and I said yes. He wanted me to meet some of his friends and co-workers. He seemed to work around the clock, so I was surprised when he asked to take me shopping. He took time off work to take me shopping and sat while the sales ladies presented him with the latest fashions in a high-end store. I didn't really like the fleece pastels prints he picked out for me. I felt like he was trying to dress me to look old. I agreed to wear the clothes he wanted when we were meeting with his friends if I could have clothes that I liked for meeting with my friends. It was a compromise. Perhaps I might have grown to like the mature outfits he had picked out for me if my cousin had not interrupted our romance.

I was lonely and after I returned from a trip to see my family. Aaron knew I was sad and suggested I invite over some family. Lexi had passed away in a car accident a few years earlier when I was incarcerated. After her death, I became closer to her brother and sister. I decided to give them a call and see if they would come visit.

Lexi's brother (Levi) and sister (Candy) came to stay for a week. One night after drinking and staying up all night, I walked into the bedroom that I shared with Aaron. To my surprise Candy was sitting naked on top of Aaron. I was shocked and closed the door and returned to the kitchen table. Candy came out and apologised I asked her why? She admitted to being jealous of the way he treated me. I let her know that we had developed our relationship over time and I really didn't think he would transfer his feelings to her so quickly from one night in bed. After a few hours, I collected my things and left. Aaron tried to stop me and apologized. I told him I was sorry. He had done so much for me and I felt indebted to him, but that was not a reason to get married. I knew deep down that I was not the right kind of girl for him. Although his love helped me heal from the hard drugs and injecting needles in my arm, I needed something more. He talked about me going to school and him paying for it. I just could not see it. My friends would be young and his would be old. How would it work? I barely knew how to communicate well, let alone go to his adult work functions and socialize. The only way it could work is if we stayed on our solitary island. When I saw him naked with my cousin, I felt sad, but not heartbroken. Maybe this was not love. Maybe these feelings were more gratitude for all he had done for me? Aaron cared deeply for me and wanted to take care of me. There was a part of me that was grateful for all he had done and taught me, but I wanted to learn to take care of myself. I could have stayed but I probably would have become stagnant and never pushed myself. He did not keep in touch with Candy. I was grateful that he did not jump into a relationship with her.

After spending time with Aaron, I no longer felt the need or desire to look for Will. Instead I looked for a job. I found one working at a laundromat. It was nothing fancy, but I was proud of myself. After months, Will found me and we hooked up again. Unfortunately, he became jealous of my work and threatened my boss. He said he thought we were having an affair. I was fired. I enjoyed honest work and being able to look at myself in the mirror. I hated scamming or cheating people out of money. Will lied and prided himself on his ability to con people out of their money. Over time I became ashamed of his lies and my lies. During one of his year long stints in jail for robbery or theft, I decided to quit with the lies. It was a very scary and hard thing to do. I lied so easily that the lies slipped out before I could stop myself. I made a commitment to myself that when I lied, I would force myself to return to the person I lied to and confess. In the beginning I told lies to survive (underage, had to say I was older). When I was older, I told lies to make my life look better than it was. It was humbling to have to admit that my tall tales were fantasies to cover up my insecurity about how I had screwed up my life. It was a necessary step to being honest with myself about where my choices had led me. Once I committed to being honest, it had a ripple effect on the people who I hung out with.

It is easy to hang out with people who lied when I was lying too. I have compassion for those who lie. I know deep down that they feel they are not good enough, or their life is not good enough. For so many years I felt like my life did not measure up to my family's standards, so I lied. Although I have compassion for this behavior, I find it uncomfortable to be around it if I can see through the lies. The other ripple effect is that you come to see yourself honestly. When I saw myself in an honest light, I did not like who I had become. There were so many people whom I admired and wanted to be like someday. They were strong, honest, independent women, with love and compassion in their hearts. I did not want to have the tough uncaring facade I was presenting to the world. My on again off again boyfriend Will, of seven years was the biggest liar I had ever met. It didn't bother me so much until I became honest around the age of 17-18.

SCHOOL

At age 18, I decided to go back to school. It was the first of many steps that helped me to fight my way out of the abusive childhood. Although I loved Will, I wanted more for my life. It was at the end of the first week of school when his patience ran out. Will gave me an ultimatum (him, or school). I chose school. When I got home later after school he was waiting with rope. He beat me and tied me up. He said he was sick of it and told me I was not going to school. Three days later when he was out for groceries, I got loose and called my aunt Emma for help. I threw a few clothes in a garbage bag and ran. The next day I went to school with two black eyes, and one was swollen shut. I explained my situation to the teachers and students. They all banded together to help me by gathering me clothes and school supplies. Most importantly, they watched for him every day and let me know if he was hanging around the front or back. They hid me and would help me get to and from school. The school was First Nations and for the first time in my life, I felt protected by an organization, that they had my best interest at heart. Later that year, I received my GED. It was the beginning of something great.

During the time I went to school, I reconnected with an Aunt Mary who allowed me to sleep on her couch and babysit her children. She was a go-getter. She had a beautiful place and a beautiful family. She lived on the main floor of a house and gave me strict rules about her drug and alcohol policy. I was incredibly grateful and admired her strength. One of the things that my mother taught me about being a good house guest was to always leave the place a little better than the way you found it. I tried to follow this rule wherever I went, anytime I was offered a sofa, or a bed.

When the top-level bachelor loft of her house became available for rent, she showed me how to fill out the application for it. I was ecstatic when I heard I could move in. This was my very first place on my own. I had rooms before on the skids, but nothing like a real place with a private kitchen and bathroom. It really meant a lot to me. Later when I graduated, she asked for donations from family members, and they chipped in to buy me shoes and a gown. I had never worn a gown and was so excited. At the grad party I had a few drinks, but no drugs. Sometime during the night, I thought it would be a good idea to go downtown to my old hangouts and make a spectacle of myself. I felt like Cinderella and didn't want the night to end. I shake my head and laugh at the silly young girl I was. I so desperately wanted validation, to be told I was special and important. I watched and learned as much as I could from my Auntie Mary. I especially appreciated her independence. Although I tried to be (independent), I had low self confidence and was unsure of myself.

On a side note, I had told my Aunt Mary that I wanted to go parachuting one day. As a graduation present, she arranged for us to go parachuting. It was one of the greatest experiences of my life. I felt like I could fly. The world slowed down, and everything made sense to me when I was in the air. I knew, come what may, I was going to be ok. This was my first jump and back then you were attached to a static line that pulled the ripcord chute as soon as you were a safe distance away from the plane. The combination of fear and joy at the same time sparked a flame inside me. Later I went back and jumped again with a new man I was dating named Steve. The outcome would be totally different.

STEVE

The difference between the first and second jump was that on the first I wanted to fly and feel that I was a part of something greater than myself. The second jump was tainted by my ego and a new boyfriend I wanted to impress. I realize that the attitude, and the energy I brought to the second jump affected the outcome.

My second jump was with a man named Steve who was tall, dark, and handsome. He asked me if I wanted to jump again and of course, I said yes. The first jump had been exhilarating. To be completely honest though, I really wanted to impress him. In my younger years I was desperate for validation from men. As with the first jump, in the morning we went through training. We were trained in the safest way to exit the plane and to count (one, one thousand, two one thousand up to six one thousand). By six one thousand the chute should have opened and if not, we pulled our emergency chute. We also learned to activate our steering by reaching up to grab the toggles and pull them down as far as we could. After training we went to the trailer to await our turn to jump. As we watched the workers folding the parachutes, we noticed a girl with a confused look on her face folding a parachute. I decided it would be best if I took the chute she folded, because I was so experienced, or ahem (full of myself). Steve was handsome and confident. I liked him immensely. As we prepared to leave the plane, my stomach did flip flops. Steve climbed out on a steel rod and pushed back as he had been instructed. I could not see him from my view, but I saw the look on the instructor's face, and he nodded when he looked out at Steve. I knew he had a good jump.

Next it was my turn. I climbed out on the steel rod and was given the signal to push off with my arms and legs. I should have been focused on making every movement perfect like on the first jump. When I pushed off, my legs did not push with the same tempo my arms did! I went into a back flip, then I was tumbling through the air. I couldn't tell which way was up or down. I saw a blur of white and grey passing by my face. Before I knew what was happening, I panicked and tried to grab onto the only thing available which was the blur in front of my face. As soon as I threw my arms around it, one of my arms ripped upwards and popped out of its socket. I screamed as I heard the pop. Again, I tumbled loosing all orientation for up or down, until finally I came to a snap in an upright position. When I recovered from the shock, I looked up to see half of my parachute open and the other half folded and tangled. I screamed toward the plane for help. For one millisecond I imagined the coach dive bombing towards me to rescue me, then I realized that was futile. My mind raced. I started to count one one thousand, two one thousand, I started to pray Dear God, there are so many things I hadn't done yet! I never married or traveled abroad! three one thousand. I was spinning because the cords were trying to untangle. My arms and legs were being pulled outwards from the gravity. Once the parachute cords untangled in one direction, the spinning force re-tangled them in the opposite direction. I tried to reach up and grab the cords to pull them apart so that it would slow the spinning. My left arm, which had been pulled from the socket, was not responding. I tried to hit my left arm with my right arm. It was useless and I could not reach it properly, because of the parachute harness. Suddenly, I felt a shudder and looked up to see three quarters of my chute now open. I knew I had to make a split decision about whether to pull my emergency ripcord! I had lost count so I wasn't sure the new one would open in time and

I was injured. If something went wrong, I would not be able to deal with it. I looked up and willed the last little bit of my chute to open. Thankfully, it opened, and I started to take stock of my surroundings. I had to figure out how I was going to get down safely. There were power lines I had to consider. I scanned the ground looking for the large orange arrow that I was supposed to aim for to maintain my direction. At first, I didn't see it because I was turned away from it. Next, I had to activate my steering toggles. My left arm would not respond. I was only able to bend it at the elbow. I could not lift it. I knew it would be harder to steer if I didn't try to pull the toggle down, so I used my right hand and reached over to pull the left toggle. I handed the left toggle to my left hand and grabbed my right toggle, pushing it all the way down to activate the steering on my right side. At least I had limited steering ability! I could not turn left, but I could turn right. The big orange arrow on the ground directed me to the left. I could not do what the orange arrow was instructing me to do. I was in horrible pain, but my adrenaline was pumping, and I had so many things to focus on to ensure the safest landing I could.

They say time slows down when you're in a life-threatening situation. I swear it felt like I was up there for at least an hour. I knew that I was going to need an ambulance for my shoulder, so hopefully, no other injuries would occur upon landing. I decided it would be best to try to get as close to the highway as I could as it would be less distance for the ambulance to travel. I did my best to steer and gage the distance and speed at which I was falling. I was so relieved that no big gusts of wind blew me off my course. As the ground rushed up to meet me, one of the ground workers ran close by.

He yelled, "What are you doing?"

I yelled back, "I need an ambulance!"

He yelled, "What?"

I yelled, "I Need A Fucking Ambulance!" The ground was coming up fast and I knew I would not be able to cinch up the chute properly to keep from travelling once I hit the ground. I put my legs together in a semi bent position. I pulled my right toggle down as far as I could to cinch up the parachute. When I hit the ground, it seemed like I bounced, as the wind caught my parachute. Suddenly I was face down and sputtering in the mud as the parachute was dragging me face down in the mud like *Super Dave Osborne*. I'm sure Steve was impressed. The ambulance brought me to the hospital in record time, since I landed so close to the road. At the hospital, the doctors and nurses held me down while they pushed my shoulder back into the socket. Luckily, they gave me a huge dose of laughing gas. Oh my God, it hurt just as much putting my arm back in the socket as it did when it was pulled out. I was given painkillers and a sling.

My relationship with Steve did not last. I admit that I was immature and insecure. I had so many insecurities and no trust. He was very stable. I was restless and unsure of my place in the world. He was a good man, but I was still very hurt and could not show or give love in a healthy way. I guess I screwed it up because I did not feel worthy.

ROBERTO

One night I met a Spanish man. I thought he was so sexy with beautiful smoldering eyes, and long eyelashes. This was my first experience of dating and he took me to fancy restaurants. On New Years Eve 1987, he offered to take me and my sister out. He rented a limousine, and we met my sister at the restaurant. His English was not the greatest, but I thought he sounded exotic. Upon meeting my sister at the table, I excused myself to use the washroom. When I arrived back at the table, my sister was visibly angry.

I asked, "What's wrong?"

She said, "He said we have the same tits."

I frowned at him and said, "Why would you say that!" He looked confused.

He replied, "I don't know what she is angry about! I said that you both have the same teeth's." He pointed at his mouth. I laughed and explained it to my sister. She took a little longer to see the humour in it. Later I would find out he was a drug dealer (Coke). I had done coke before, but not a lot, as it was expensive. I had struggled to get off the needles (T's & R's) so it wasn't long before I added coke to the list of substances, that I became addicted to. I moved in with him for a brief period and was his mule. He did the deals, and I packed the drugs. Most nights I hung out in the bar with girlfriends snorting in the bathroom. Some nights he and I shut down early and got high. That was a big mistake because we would be behind the eight ball and have to make up the money we snorted. The more drugs we did, the more we fought, until I moved out. He had snapped some pictures of me when I was high. He tried to use them to entice me to come home one night. I think they were the worst pictures I've ever seen of myself. I ripped them up thinking that I looked terrible, like death. My face was grey and gaunt from not eating healthily or adequately. My eyes looked empty. That enraged him and he spat at me and told me he should have turned me out! I went crazy and attacked him. All we did was fight. I don't know why he wanted to be with me. It was a hard relationship to leave because of the addiction. When I went out with my girlfriends, he pretended to hug me and slip me a couple of grams. Then he just waited until after I got high. He knew I would come find him to get more. It was my girlfriends and cousins and sister Samantha that helped me to stay away from him. When I went out, I was with them and they reminded me of how awful he treated me and how we fought. Over time his charm and the drugs lost their spell over me. When I saw those pictures of me, it helped me to realize how crazy I looked.

One night in a weak moment, I hooked up with him. I learned a few weeks later I was pregnant. I do not know why I told him; I think it was out of a sense of duty. I tried to imagine my life with him, and all I saw was drug induced fights. I imagined me struggling to look after a child with disabilities due to the cocaine. Drugs had been the glue that held our relationship together. It seemed like a very bleak future.

He started to make plans. We would move in with his mom and get married. He became so bossy and overbearing that I knew I could not live with him. I was terrified. I knew he would take control of my life. The gang that he hung around who had previously stayed in the background became hostile towards me and let me know that they view me as his property. I told him that I have not figured out what I'm going to do yet. One night in a panic, I called Will and told him I wanted to have coffee. We met and I explained that I was pregnant and didn't know what to do. He offered to take care of me and the baby. I knew that was not an option. Roberto would only let me have freedom if he wasn't the father of my child. I decided the best decision for me was to have an abortion. Will escorted me to the clinic. It was a heartbreaking moment in my life. I was wracked with guilt and pain. Will took me home and took care of me for a week. The guilt and pain I carried would haunt me for years to come. Through this experience, I learned the value of life and vowed never to do that again. I thank the little spirit who came to taught me and lived with me for a short period.

Roberto was livid and threatening. I had not realized he was so religious, until he left bibles on my door with highlighted passages about women obeying men. He also painted a big black cross on my door. I was not sure what that meant?

GRANDMOTHER

A month after the abortion my grandmother Ellie fell ill, and all of the family were summoned to the hospital back at Ryan's Creek. Ironically, my grandfather Leon was also there, but most of my family were not speaking to him or visiting with him. I did my best to avoid any questions regarding my pregnancy. Family members quickly realized that I was no longer pregnant and that it was an uncomfortable topic. Although my father forbade me to visit my grandfather Leon, I could not listen. My father's parents were always loving and kind to me. They always told me I was special and made me feel important. Sadly, my grandmother passed away. Her passing served to further drive home the value of life. It was an exceedingly difficult time for everyone in my family. As a result of her passing, I was away a lot longer than I had anticipated. Many family members, including myself, had a hard time dealing with her loss. I stayed to help with the funeral as best as I could.

CLEANED OUT

I had left Will at my place during the funeral. I was concerned because he was becoming controlling, and belligerent. He let me know that if I didn't get home soon, I would be sorry. In truth, I was scared to go home. What was there to go back to? I had done it again and jumped from the kettle into the frying pan. Will was no better than Roberto. I had selfishly used Will to get rid of Roberto. I hadn't yet realized that when you had a place you had to take care of it. A concept that was unfamiliar to me. My father was trying to convince me to stay and hang out with him for a month at his place on Lox Creek Reservation. He bought me a television set for my graduation a few months prior that I thought Will would take and pawn off. Although my dad said it did not matter to him, it mattered to me. I had truly done little adulting in my life and was hoping to become more responsible. My Aunt Mary had trusted me and helped me get that place and I didn't want to let Will mess that up for me. I was worried he would throw a party and become violent, as that was his normal behavior. Sadly, Will had a bigger surprise waiting for me. When I returned home, everything including clothing, furniture, dishes, and wall pictures were gone. He even took the toilet paper from the bathroom! How vindictive! At first, I felt like I deserved it. Later, I became angry. It was my first real place on my own! Someday when I saw him again, I vowed he would get it.

For many years, I still gravitated to skid row. My low self

esteem pulled me back to my safe comfort zone. However, there were many places that I thought I wasn't able to enter. It seems funny to me now. I remembered being invited to a Red Robin (a burger joint) for a birthday party. I got to the address, when I arrived there, I assessed the place as too fancy. There was a lot of beautiful red velvet fabric and shiny brass in the decor. I watched the party from outside for a while before I turned and walked away.

REVENGE

One day, out of the blue, Will called. He said he had done a big score and had five thousand dollars. I was still pissed at him for stealing all of my furniture. He was charming towards me and acted like he had done nothing wrong. He invited me downtown to a skid row bar to drink. I asked if he minded if my sister Samantha, came as well and he agreed. We all met at the bar and drank highballs and shots of tequila. After a couple of hours, I asked him to get us a hotel room upstairs. He agreed and I told Samantha that I would be down shortly. Once we got to the room, we had a few more drinks. Then, after he passed out, I pulled off all his clothes, took his money and left to go down to the bar. I told Samantha we have to leave now. She asked me what happened, and I told her that I had rolled him. I threw his clothes in a garbage on the street. I share this with you because I don't want to just paint a picture of a girl who was a victim. I did my share of bad things and I was no innocent angel. Somewhere along the rugged path I had taken, I learned to push back. Perhaps in the beginning, I was a child and didn't know better. In my older years, I was revengeful and could be petty. That night, we drank to our hearts content, toasting Will.

NATHAN

Eventually, I gave up the hard drugs and got a job at a bar as a coat check girl. The bar was located just off the skid row. I still knew a lot of dealers. When they gifted me any drugs, I sold them to make a little extra. I was able to cut back on drinking, to only once or twice a month. I tried to stay out of relationships and refused to date. I was tired of men. I was struggling financially, just scraping by, but I was peaceful.

One night after the bar closed when I was leaving and the other workers were having their usual nightcap, I saw a man getting beaten up by a few other guys. He asked if he could come in and wait till the guys were gone, so I let him in the bar. He was drunk and a little belligerent. He said his name was Nathan. After I rescued him, we went to an after-hours party, and met up with my sister Samantha. After a few drinks I invited him back to my place and we hooked up. I was intrigued that he had a job and savings. I had never been in a relationship with a guy who was somewhat respectable. They didn't seem to look my way. Six months after meeting Nathan I was pregnant.

Once pregnant with my daughter Destiny, Nathan became very possessive. He threw tantrums and broke things. He forbade me to go downtown to the skids or maintain any of my prior friendships with co-workers from the bar. This would be the final break from all of the skid rows I had gravitated to my whole life. All I had ever wanted was to be loved and to feel deeply connected with someone. I had felt alone and unworthy of love all my life and I hoped that Nathan and Destiny would fill the void. I vowed to work as hard as I could to be the best mother in the world. This angered Nathan.

He told me I had changed, and he didn't like it. I started to read books on pregnancy and babies in the first year. I so desperately wanted to be a good mother and prayed Nathan would be a good father and husband. During my pregnancy it became clear that his violence was not just a passing phase. The violence started when I was pregnant. When he attacked me, I shielded Destiny by putting my stomach in the corner, so that he hit my back. I forgave myself for staying with him because I needed to have something or someone to hold onto, even if they treated me badly. There was a part of me that believed it was my fault and that I deserved it. I traded the streets and addiction for this abusive man. Destiny was a precious diamond in our rough life that made it all worthwhile.

TREATMENT

After being violently attacked by Nathan one summer night, I managed, thankfully, to convince him to get help with his drinking and go to a drug and alcohol treatment centre. I believed that if I could only get him to stop drinking, the violence would end, and we could be a happy family. We applied to go into a couple's treatment centre for six weeks. When he didn't show up at the treatment centre and I was preparing to leave, a counsellor convinced me to stay. She believed I needed it just as much as him. At the time I did not think so, because I thought the problem was him. The program was six weeks of intensively looking at myself, as well as some one to one counselling. We also did a lot of self reflection exercises and sharing circle work. It is funny how it was both healing, and scary to share my story. While in treatment, I shared the story about the abuse I had suffered from my mother when I wet the bed. It was a very heavy circle, and we were given a break to get some air, or a cigarette. I was a smoker and was outside smoking when an older lady approached me and asked me if I knew who she was. I did not.

She said, "As I listened to your story, I was transported back to when I was a little girl back in Residential School. I watched your mother brutally beaten in the same way you had described in your childhood." So many lightbulbs went off. I thought that my mother hated me and lay in bed at night dreaming up cruel ways to hurt me. At the time, I knew very little about how First

Nations children were forced to attend the Residential School. Most children had such traumatic experiences that they could not talk about them their whole lives. "A popular belief in both the scholarly and popular literature is that adults who were abused as children are more likely to abuse their children" (National Research Council 1993). The sad part is that healing comes from sharing our stories. So many live with this pain locked away inside their hearts. For so long I had believed it was my fault. I thought I deserved the cruelty my mother inflicted upon me. To find out she was hurt in the same way somehow helped me to challenge the belief that I deserved the violence inflicted upon me as a child. Once I realized the truth, that it was not my fault, I began to look for safe people and places to heal.

It was scary for me to leave a situation that was so violent. It was not easy to walk away from the fantasy of a happy life with Destiny's father. But ultimately, I knew I wanted my daughter to grow up with a love that did not include physical pain. It took baby steps to find my sense of safety, and to get help. I didn't do it alone. I began the healing journey away from violence once I found a sense of safety in friends and counsellors. Slowly I began sharing stories about my painful past. I would love to say it was a smooth transition and I never went back, but that would be a lie. It took a few years to finally close the door to the abuse. After many years of counselling, I began to write about the childhood experiences of violence that impacted my self worth.

Throughout my life I had lived with a lot of chaos and fear. Perhaps I became addicted to the adrenaline and my distorted sense of fear. After I escaped the violence of my upbringing, I gravitated to dangerous people and places. In my own healing journey, the most important step for me was to learn to find safety and to become accustomed to the feeling of peace. Growing up in chaos taught me to feel comfortable with it. I envied those that seemed to live peaceful lives. Unfortunately, when I found myself in a peaceful atmosphere, l felt restless. It was hard to acclimatize and to accept peace and enjoy it. It did not come easily or quickly. For me it was a gradual process that took time and patience.

The few years I spent living on the streets were hard. I do not deny it. I also do not deny the times I was offered help and did not take it or the drugs I sought, to relieve the pain. I know that it was my path, and I chose it. I am terribly sorry for those I hurt during those years. I still face many challenges today and I would like to think I'm getting better at facing them. The development of healthy boundaries for me, is a huge accomplishment. I am grateful to my spirit for helping me to take the time to be silent and find respectful ways to say, "No thank you."

Sometimes when I feel that I am under attack. Logically, I know this is not the case because the experience I am walking into is a growth enhancing one, such as speaking in public or going to a job interview. I will chant these mantras over and over in my mind. I am safe, I am loved, I am protected. The Creator has a plan for me, and it is, greater than any plan I could have for myself. I also find that slowing my breath down at the same time helps to enhance the feeling of safety. I breathe in for a count of four and breathe out for a count of seven.

Fear can show up in many ways. It can keep us safe when we are in danger or it can be an unhealthy by-product of severe trauma in childhood and the absence of connection to loving caregivers. It can also be the debilitating face of Complex Post Traumatic Stress Disorder. After living with fear throughout my life, I have learned to understand and identify which fear I am up against in each situation. As a child, I disassociated from fear because of all the violence I had endured. I was fearless as a youth, caring little for the precious life I was given. For periods of time in my healing journey, I suffered from CPTSD and tackled debilitating irrational fears and phobias. As I healed, I learned to reconnect, and listen to my fear receptors.

Intuition is the little voice inside of you. Never try to silence that little voice inside of you when you hear it. It could save your life one day. As a child, I looked to adults to protect me and teach me how to be safe. Sadly, my parents had suffered abuse and were not able to pass that wisdom on to me.

Over the course of my life, I have come to believe that counselling is a life saving tool. I could not be who I am without learning to share my story. Counselling taught me to open up and trust and share.

The first step in learning to stay safe against violence was recognizing it. People wondered how I could go back to the men who were abusing me. I knew firsthand that it was not because I enjoyed the pain in any way shape or form. Over time, I realized that my poor definition of love was instilled in me as a child. I learned that in order to receive love, I must accept a certain amount of pain. I desperately wanted to be loved. While other girls got butterflies in their stomach, I got knots in mine. The knots and tension became a part of me that I did not know how to function without. I felt empty and alone without those knots. With the help of counselling and sharing circles each subsequent relationship became less violent than the previous one. I am happy to say that I married a man who has never raised a hand to me.

Most of my fears nowadays are growth enhancing as I learn to push past the comfortable safe space I have created in my mind and open myself up to new teachings. Sharing my heart and story is one way I push myself past and through my comfort zone.

Everyday I walk towards the uncomfortable to meet life with humbleness and gratitude for the path before me. Nelson Mandela said it best. "Courage is not the absence of fear, but the triumph over it. The brave man is not he who does not feel afraid, but he who conquers that fear". One of the scariest, most rewarding accomplishments has been to face my past and look within.

There are still many unwritten chapters in my life, but I really wanted to focus on the kidnapping, the events that led me to homelessness and extreme drug use, as well as the long slow path back from it. There may be some out there that may have similar stories and that can identify with my journey. Many have asked how I came back from the trauma, addictions, and street life. There was no one incident that flipped a switch for me. It was a gradual process of learning to trust and ask for help. The many people that saw something good in me and offered me a hand are my heroes. I would not be where I am without them. In my experience, it was connections to others that healed me. The more I put up walls and walked away from people, the lonelier I became and the more I gravitated to harder and stronger drugs. When I learned to trust individuals that wanted to help me, I began the path back from escaping into the drugs, and alcohol.

GRANNY ELLIE

On a final note, I have wrestled with how much to share about the special relationship I shared with my Granny Ellie. During my reckless youth, I stopped by to visit my father on the reservation. Usually, it was when I was either fleeing a violent relationship or trying to dry out, or detox myself for a bit. I was seventeen at the time and my restless spirit was ready to go again. I was ready to either hitchhike out or hop a train. I was walking around town to see if there might be anyone around who was going to the city. My grandmother happened to see me since she was on her way to bingo. She called me over to her car and told me to get in.

She said, "I'll give you a ride."

I told her, "I'm going to the City. It is ok Granny. You can let me off. I'll be alright". Granny Ellie pulled over to the side of the road.

She said, "I want to buy you a train ticket." She must have heard of the dangerous ways I travelled and did not want to leave me like that. I was weary. I was not sure why she would do that. Although I loved her, I was a little intimidated by her. She tanned hides and was an extremely hard worker. I did not know how to talk to her. I felt odd around her, like a broken toy. She seemed to look at the world in a different way that I could not understand.

She told me she would buy me a train ticket and give me $60, which was a lot back then (early 80's), if I would sit and listen to her until the train came. I agreed, even though I was nervous. She drove me to the train. As she hobbled into the train station and bought my ticket, I thought, oh no what have I got myself into? It was three hours before the train would come. At first, we made small talk and she shared some dried salmon and dried elk with me. She told me some stories of the old days of people and times gone by. It was warm and comforting in her car. I felt safe for a while. As the time neared for my train to arrive, she pulled out her wallet and gave me the promised $60.

As she handed it to me, she said, "I know you are going to spend this money on drugs. I just want you to promise me one thing?" I was a little shocked that she was being so forthright. I was not entirely sure I could make that promise to her.

She said, "I know you've been hurt so much in your life already. I want you to promise me that when you do the drugs or use alcohol with this money," She paused, then added, "promise me you will keep yourself safe. Don't get so wasted that you put yourself in danger, please!"

I was shocked and said, "Yes of course Granny I can make you that promise." Those words would stay with me all my life. The unconditional love she showed me would last a lifetime. She is gone but I still see her in my dreams, and she helps me from the spirit world.

The other thing she said was, "Do you remember when you were a small child, maybe you were four or five. I looked after you for a few days, just you! We took a trip?"

I said, "Vaguely, not so much." At first my mind was blank, but It came back to me. She and I had driven for days.

She said, "You had told me back then you would be taken by a bad man when you got older". She also said, "Do you remember talking to the spirits when you were young?"

I told her, "I only remember one."

She said, "The spirits told you that you would be taken by a man and he would hurt you." I remember I had an imaginary

141

friend, and everyone made fun of me. Everyone, that is, except granny Ellie. His name was Michael. She was the only one who believed in Michael, based on what Michael told me to tell her, she took me on a distant trip to ask for help for me.

I only remember a small part of the ceremony. It is hot, I am dressed in a long cotton gown, I am trying to sit like her with my legs to the side. We are on a bed of cedar. It is hot, and I tell her, it is hard to breathe. She tells me to lay down, and she helps me. Her hands are gentle, and cool. After I lay down, she strokes my hair. The air is cool and sweet. I am safe, loved and protected. She says that they worked on me to help fix my future road. The outcome of this ceremony is between those who are present and the spirits, as our ceremonial protocols prescribe. What I do know and share with certainty is, I am thankful for my granny's love and teachings and I am thankful to be alive today!

Later when we were driving back, the car broke down, and she jacked it up. It was the front right tire, and the car was pointed downhill. For some reason she crawled under the car to look at something while it was jacked up. She had a bum leg, and it was hard for her to maneuver to see whatever it was she was trying to look at.

Michael told me, "Tell her to get out!" I tried to but she would not listen.

He said, "She is going to get hurt really badly, if you don't get her out."

I started to scream, "Granny get out! you're going to get hurt really badly, get out of there!" I pulled her, but she was too big. She scrambled out from under the car just in time. It fell off the jack. If she had been under there she would have been crushed. She was a little shaken, and I was crying.

She asked me, "Did he tell you?". I nodded yes. She called him a spirit. I called him Michael.

Remembering those events have haunted me from time to

time. They are like a trail of breadcrumbs down a dark forest path. Do I dare to see where they might lead? Am I strong enough?

The train is boarding, I hop out of the station wagon that doubles as a hotel room when she is traveling. She travels a lot on her own. I admire that about her. To me, she seems fearless. I give her a quick hug and I am off. I don't really know how to make sense of what she said at the time, I file it in my memory bank and will cherish this memory in my later years. I am grateful for all her help, as well as for those who cared enough to pray for protection over me.

EPILOGUE

Thank you, Creator, for blessing me, in so many ways, and for the chance to love you, and the world in a deeper more connected way.

I was asked, 'If I could go back in time to design a healthy plan for myself as a child, what would it look like? This is what I have come up with.

1) A safe place to take two or three months to process the feeling of safety. Any child who has been hurt so much needs time to acclimatize to the feeling of safety. Trust cannot be built in a week. To begin to feel safe enough to trust and open up, I needed time. It seemed the primary concern was to get me into school. School can be important later. Learning cannot take place if you do not feel safe. It would be good to have some time to be quiet and alone, maybe connect to nature or animals, dogs, or horses. It is too hard to trust humans in the beginning. Maybe some type of music or art therapy to begin with would be helpful.

2) The most important thing you can say to a person who has suffered trauma is, that it is not your fault, and I believe you. I so needed to hear that from my parents and anyone that I met immediately after. I believed it was my fault all my life and have struggled with self hatred

as a result. My mother attended residential school from age 2- 16. She was not given the loving nurturing skills needed to be a parent, or to prevent and deal with any part of the kidnapping. I forgive her completely. I do not know if I could have survived her life. She never stopped looking for me. Kirk was wrong when he said nobody cared and nobody was looking for me. She loved me with all of her heart.

3) Any child who has been sexually abused needs to be able to learn healthy boundaries with respect to their body. Either they never learned to begin with, or their boundaries are stripped away by the abuse. Now I can recognize that Dave and Kirk sexually abused me. I did not know this as a child. I had no language for the emotions I felt at the time because I was taught at a young age to be seen and not heard. It has been a long road to connect with and process the emotional damage I suffered.

It is important to allow your child to say no to people they don't feel comfortable around. If a child is never allowed to say no to adults, there is an extremely high risk that they will become victims to predatory adults. So many of us native children are taught to respect our Elders. This includes being forced to hug elders when we do not want to. This reinforces in us the belief that we don't have the right to ownership over our bodies and personal space. Sometimes, this opened the door to abuse. I thought I was the only one in my family. I was wrong and have since learned that many family members, an alarming number, in fact, were the victim of sexual abuse.

My father tried to ignore what had happened for quite awhile. The message I got from this behavior was that he didn't care or maybe he was in denial. One day, out of the blue, he tried to talk to me about the birds and the bees. I became enraged because I believed this to be a symptom of his denial. What do you think happened while I was gone? Do you think we just held hands? I walked away. Sadly, I think it was his attempt at teaching me healthy boundaries regarding my body. The relationship between my father and I was damaged by the kidnapping, and by the fact that my dad was not able to show emotion. As a result, we were estranged for many years. I forgave him because I know he was trying to protect his heart. The birth of my daughter opened that door between us.

4) When the child has learned to feel safe and supported. It is important to speak about sexuality in an open healthy way. A child needs to understand that it is normal for them to experience sexual feelings when they are being inappropriately touched by someone. This can be so confusing for the child. When Dave started touching and licking my private parts at age eight, he activated my sexual hormones. Even though I did not want my body to react, and I stayed as still as I could. My physical body still reacted, with a racing heart, dizziness, and tingling sensations. The sexual part of my mind was woken up at a young age. My sexual brain was programed to fight against enjoying the act of sex.

The first sexual pleasure responses in your body can imprint in your brain and leave you with desires that may seem unnatural. For me, these desires were like a shameful demon in my head that I could never share with anyone. Feeling these body sensations added to my sense of guilt, and shame. Also, a child needs to be taught to distinguish the difference between love and sex, because they are not the same. They need to learn that they do not have to submit to sex because they want love. I suffered a lot because I had to learn this in the school of hard knocks.

One of the important tools that I learned through this journey was that I am not my body, I am not my mind and I am not my emotions. my spirit is eternal. My spirit is where my strength is. Learning to connect to my spirit is the strongest tool I used to help me walk through the fire and look back at my painful childhood. I learned to sit in those excruciatingly uncomfortable memories that brought overwhelming emotions. At times, I was not sure I could live through them again. Sometimes the pain I experienced while writing this story was so unbearable, I felt like giving up. At times, the emotional pain manifested itself into physical pain. My hands burned and I had to plunge them in cold water and ice, because they felt so hot. Also, while writing this book I also developed a tumor in my womb that had to be removed. Luckily, it was not cancerous but, it did leave me wondering whether the tumour would have turned on me if I had not allowed myself to keep going and let the shame and guilt I felt go. I pray that this will reach you in love and light.

A male friend asked me once, "Do you think it is important for me to take my little girl to church?" I replied, "I think it is important to teach your child at a young age that there is a higher power at work that she can call upon. Whether you use the church or yourself or a different religion, is up to you. Someday she will not have you and she will eventually face some insurmountable odds." We all do. "She will be able to thank the Creator/God in the good times, as well as call out to God/Creator to help her to make it through the bad. You will also find some peace in knowing she has that connection."

I could not be who I am, or I could not have made it through without my faith in God/Creator.

The biggest gift my father gave me was teaching me, years later when I had succumbed to the hardest of drugs, and the vilest types of alcohol, that I could pray, and that the Creator would hear my prayers. I was worthy. I forgive my father completely. I know now that he did his best.

AFTERWARD

This book started out as just a healing tool for me, but turned into a book. Now I realize the power in learning to love and accept myself. When I lived on the streets dealing and using drugs, I witnessed a lot of people in pain. People die daily from violence or drug abuse. I have watched the skid rows of North America become larger and larger over the years. It is my hope that this book can help those who work with sexual abuse trauma survivors or are the parents of sexually abused children, to understand some of their struggles they may be needing help with. If you are the survivor, I say to you: It is not your fault. I Love you, and you are Loved. The Creator/God loves you. I believe in you. You can find a safe place to heal, because you are stronger than you know. Try to keep yourself safe when you are using whichever drugs or alcohol is your choice. The Creator/God will hear your prayer even when you are high or intoxicated. One day, you will start your journey back from the pain. My wish for you is that, from this day forward, you will add no more hurt and pain onto your already full plate. Figure out what makes you happy in a healthy way (reading, happy movies, listening, or playing music, drawing, writing, working out, walking in nature), so that when you are sinking (the memories are overtaking you), you can use these tools to pull yourself out. Creator please help those who might benefit find this book and bless them.

I have worked so hard to overcome my past, but that does

not mean I don't get angry and irritable at times. I still must work through triggers. I am still a work in progress. I know now that forgiveness is the key for me. I forgive myself even though I can't remember it all. I have wondered at times if I can forgive even though there was no remorse or apology? Can I forgive even when I sometimes feel afraid, sad and alone? It has taken me forever to get here. I always thought that I would need to be at a place where the feelings had subsided to be able to forgive the men that sexually abused me as a child. For me it has been the opposite, the traumatic pain I lived with has subsided since I made up my mind to forgive. I do not say all need to forgive, everyone has a right to hold on to whatever painful experiences they have endured. I arrived at this place after years of holding on to my pain. Although I have done my best to let go of what I remember there are still pieces lurking in my mind.

Even though I sleep so much better, I sometimes still wake in fear and anxiety to the sound of a gun going off. My brother, my mother and the police all said Kirk had a gun. The fear I feel when I wake to the sound of the gun is indescribable. I wake gasping for breath. Thank god, it doesn't happen very often.

Gandhi, Nelson Mandela, and His Holiness the Dalai Lama inspire me to forgive even though I must admit there is still some fear.

I have found in my quest to forgive that there are different levels:

1) Able to talk about the painful experience, but still harbour anger and resentment, but have not gone back to reconnect with the pain. (I spent many years here).
2) Have gone back and reconnected with the pain and processed memories and am able to have compassion. (This is where I am now).
3) Able to grow and use the pain to help make the world a better place. (This is where I wish to be).

I have compassion for Kirk and the person he was when he took me. His intent was to save me. Sadly, he could only break me because he was broken. I forgive him for the pain he inflicted upon me as a child. In his own messed up way, he thought he was rescuing me. I forgive Dave for I know he felt guilt for what he was doing to me. I choose to forgive. To release the hurt and pain, I had to go back and look at the experiences in the light of day with no mind-altering substances to distort the memories. I have walked through the fire and made peace with who I was and the role I played in my kidnapping. I pray for all the men who hurt me to learn to connect with the Creator in the hopes that they may spread a healthier type of love in the world. As you can imagine, I have had to overcome many destructive behavior patterns to become who I am now. If you are trying to overcome something huge, I say, please reach out and ask for help. Although I thought I was alone, I was not. God/Creator was and is always with me. Many people showed up at pivotal moments in my life to help. Now I can see there are no coincidences. The Creator sends us helpers in all sizes, shapes, colours, and religions.

Many events would shape the course of my life following my painful childhood and the biggest and most prominent being the birth of my daughter. If only I knew back then, what I know now. I am sure every parent feels the same way. Recently, I returned to school, although I had a great job, and made great money, I felt a yearning to understand more about how I arrived at this place. I had raised an unhappy child who felt anger and resentment towards me. Was it supposed to be that way? The few books I'd read said, no. I could not blame it on anyone else. I was the one responsible for showing her love and how to get along in the world. Unfortunately, most of what I learned was from counselling and books. I admit, I am ill equipped to be a loving and supportive mother. Mentally, I was distracted by my pain and it showed up in dissociative ways and emotionally, I was shut down. I gave my daughter little praise, few hugs or kind loving supportive words. Many times, my outbursts were volatile and irrational. My love for her, caused her pain and for this I am eternally sorry. It is my hope that the more I learn, and connect with the Creator, the planet (mother earth), her people, and myself, the more I will learn to show her love in a healthier way. As I look back, I am able to find acceptance for the girl I once was, and who did her best. Growing up I knew extraordinarily little about Residential Schools or First Nations history. All I remember was being taught in school that we were savages, and that I was a squaw. I was ashamed of who I was. It took many years of searching to make peace with who I am and understand the legacy of our people. Those that lived in the school that my mother attended endured horrible abuses at the hands of the nuns and priests. They were starved, beaten, sexually abused, and forced to endure hard labour. They were raised without the love and support of their parents who cared about them.

The children in the residential schools were under the complete control of their sexual abusers, and there was no one they could tell. Many grew up and never spoke of their residential school experience, even though they spent their entire young life there. My mother was there from age two to sixteen. I can count on one hand the times she spoke about that place.

I bring up these facts to put into context the intergenerational trauma among First Nation in Canada. Since 1867, when the first schools were opened, 154 years have passed. We now can see across Canada the devastating effects that Residential Schools have had upon First Nations peoples. At times, the task of helping so many may seem daunting. How do we help so many with Attachment disorders, Complex Post Traumatic Stress, and Dissociative disorders?

Many have looked to their traditional cultural teachings, in hopes that the healing will come from rituals and ceremonies. This has been a turning point for First Nations. For, we are erasing the colonial assumption that our culture holds no value in the world. Many are waking up and remembering who we were before the imposition of European influences wreaked havoc upon our shores. Those who have had the courage to come forward and speak of the horrors of Residential Schools and lead us out of the dark, should be commended. Additionally, those who lived and did their best to bring up their children despite their tragic pasts, deserve our love and respect. Healing, for First Nations peoples, must be done with the utmost care and responsibility, in that I mean we are responsible to be the light in the dark for all to see. We must take the time for self-care and learn to live healthy balanced lives to the best of our ability. Most importantly, we must be compassionate with ourselves and all our relations. We must accept each other's struggles and that we are all doing the best we can.

I see my people. They are kind, loving, resilient, and incredibly strong people who share a deep and personal love of nature, and the planet. We are all connected to people, plants, animals, mother earth in all her forms, the universe, and the Creator. In these pages I make sense of the suffering of my people and rise above my own individual trauma to try to look at the bigger picture, as well as, to try to find the way forward with this new knowledge. I know without a doubt, we cannot heal anyone until we heal ourselves.

We must find the courage to tell our stories if we are to use our stories to help us grow. We must share them, otherwise, they are just shameful secrets holding us back. We might think we have escaped our past, but until we let our secrets out into the open, they live in our minds controlling and dictating our lived experience.

In conclusion, if you have not suffered through physical and sexual assault or if you are not First Nations; it is my hope this story, helps you to see beyond the stereotypes of all my relations, my beautiful First Nation's brothers, and sisters.

Kintsugi is the Japanese art of repairing broken pottery with lacquer dusted or mixed with powdered gold, silver, or platinum. The pottery piece evolves into something more beautiful as it's cracks are highlighted, rather than hidden.

My memories were distorted, and I felt broken because they were so jumbled. I struggled to piece them together in a linear fashion. I felt broken and it is ok. I could not become the loving compassionate being I am today, without breaking. I have found the beauty in my brokenness.

All My Relations.

ABOUT THE AUTHOR

Sky is a First Nations woman. She is a true survivor. She has overcome her adversities and empowered herself so that she can help others wo are struggling. She is a strong and dynamic woman who focuses on the road ahead, fueled by her traumatic experiences.

Printed in the United States
by Baker & Taylor Publisher Services